1984

The ABC's of Developing Software

The ABC's of Developing Software

A Primer on
Essentials of Software Development

Sheldon D. Softky, Ph.D.

Cartoons by Randy Everson

Menlo Park
The ABC Press of Silicon Valley

The contents of this book are the author's opinion about general practices in the software industry. They are not represented as the policies or practices of any particular company.

"PDL" is a registered trademark of Caine, Farber, & Gordon, Inc., Pasadena, California.

Distributed by William Kaufmann, Inc., 95 First Street, Los Altos, California 94022

Library of Congress Cataloging in Publication Data

Softky, Sheldon D., 1926–
    The ABCs of developing software.

    Bibliography: p.
    1. Electronic digital computers—Programming.
I. Title.   II. Title: ABCs of developing software.
QA76.6.S6168   1983   001.64'2   83-7051
ISBN 0-912957-00-X

Printed in the United States of America

Contents

SECTION 1
Confronting a New Software Project

Chapter 1. The Big Questions   1

> What do we need?
> What have we got?
> What do we have to produce?
> How and when do we produce it?

SECTION 2
Resources Needed

Chapter 2. People   7

> All the staff can't do the work as a form of on-the-job training, but it is
> amazing how a few real experts can help everyone else if the management
> will let them.

Chapter 3. Writing and Publishing Capabilities   11

> Software requires producing mostly written text, so equipment and
> organization are necessary.

Chapter 4. Computer Hardware and Terminals   13

> The computer has to be there and be accessible.

Chapter 5. Automated Development Aids   17

> Compilers, text editors, design language editors, data definition systems
> are important needs.

SECTION 3
The Products of Software Development

SECTION 4
The Phases of Software Development

Foreword

Software originally meant only a collection of a few computer programs. The functions performed were simple, and individual programs could be written independently. Now, however, these programs have to be part of a *software product* that performs elaborate functions. The programs must be integrated pieces of the product and must reliably work together. Instead of *programming*, it is *software engineering* that generates software products in a formal project environment.

In large hardware systems (such as process plants, ground-control stations, and satellites) the role of software is to allow the user to find status and to control the hardware. Traditionally, this software was built by directly translating each function into programs. How these programs must fit together was left to the last stage of development. With this approach, it frequently took years to produce a workable system. Ironically, by the time the system was delivered to the user, it was found that it didn't perform properly because of functions which were altered or omitted to get the system to work. The approach that cured this problem was to fully design the software system "from the top, down" so that the integration of program functions was in the design before any programs were written. In most projects this required that the people who engineered the software have major training in the events and products of the project.

In the software project all professional personnel need training in the correct sequence of activities necessary to design and code the software by structured methods: namely, the analysis of functions from the most general to the most specific (*top-down analysis*). Separate training in each of these methods is easily available, but how do they fit together to make a successful project? This book will help to answer this question.

Software engineers are generally trained in the uses of modern techniques in a laboratory environment, not a project environment. In the lab the software engineer generates a program to perform a specific function. He tests the program to show that it works and devotes little effort to how this one program fits together with others; this product then has little documentation for the user's benefit and comes with no formal guarantee.

In the project environment the software product is more formally conceived. It is designed, generated, tested, and documented. Points of interaction with other programs and major design decisions are made early in the project. Standards that all software engineers must adhere to are defined. The software is rigorously tested. What are the procedures of the software project? What are the products of software engineering? How these disciplines are implemented and how the project environment determines the generation of the software are examined in *The ABC's of Developing Software*.

This book describes the software engineering products, how these products are produced, and why they should be produced. A discussion then follows on how these products are used by the software personnel to engineer the software product.

For software project managers and software engineers this book will assist in the training, or retraining, of software personnel in the software engineering discipline. All project personnel will be enlightened as to the concepts and requirements of software engineering. Finally, *ABC's* delves into the modern techniques of software engineering and the events and documentation required to engineer a software product.

Most computer science curricula teach the tools of software engineering but not the concept of software engineering as a whole. Further, computer science students generate software in the lab environment, not the project environment. Consequently, for the computer science instructor or student this book introduces an integrated approach to software engineering. It describes the phases of a software project including, in particular, the formal and rigorous testing of the software in order to produce a software product. The phases of a software project and how the tools of software engineering are used to produce a successful software product are the primary topics of *The ABC's of Developing Software*.

—Larry Hinman
Saratoga, California
December 1982

Acknowledgments

I owe a debt of gratitude to Bob Axtell for his continuing encouragement and his suggestions as a reviewer and to Sylvan Rubin for all his valuable advice, for his use as a sounding board for my opinions, and for his reviews. I appreciate the encouragement and approval of Gene Leonard; the enthusiasm of Bob Burke as a reviewer; the clever cartoons of Randy Everson; and the inspiration of Larry Hinman, who convinced me that I should write this book. Finally, I especially feel grateful to my two technical editors, my wife, Marion, and Sunny Olds, for performing a trying chore with magnificent patience and competence.

—SDS

The Ten Commandments
of Software Development

I. Honor thy requirements, both in the creation of them and in their satisfaction by the software.

II. Treat any proposed schedule as a potential serpent, because it can bite thee where thou allow not for contingencies.

III. Look upon the project documents as thy friends in time of need, and so prepare them with respect.

IV. "An ounce of insight is worth a pound of motivation," therefore begrudge not the time spent on training.

V. Honor thy people and reward them with encouragement, because it is only they who produce the software.

VI. Remember always that the software will be used and repaired by people, so keep them in mind when design is started.

VII. Design, and verify its goodness, before writing any programs.

VIII. Regard design as a process of gaining insight; therefore be willing to design and redesign till insight is complete.

IX. The three most important features of software design are modularity, modularity, and modularity.

X. Be not afraid of testing, because if thy design is good, testing will be easy.

"BUZZWORDS" IN SOFTWARE ENGINEERING

Analysis
To figure out how the system should work

"Bottom-Up"
To analyze system functions at the simplest level without figuring out how they have to fit together within the whole system

Documentation
All of the plans, schedules, standards, program descriptions, and procedures produced as documents to support software engineering work and to describe programs

Requirements
The written statements that formally specify what the software must do or how it must be structured

Reviews
Official customer evaluations of the work performed to date on software

Software
The computer's instructions

Software Product
The software that is formally developed to meet a set of requirements

Software Engineering
The activity of producing the software product in a formal project environment

Structured Analysis
To analyze a system by decomposing general functions into less general ones, until all are expressed as simple functions

Structured Design
To design a system so that general functions are implemented by less general ones, until all are implemented as simple functions

Top-Down Design
To start with the top-level functions of a system and design, advancing to progressively greater levels of detail

Introduction

This book is about the way that software is developed. It is about an activity called *software engineering*, an area where most of the effort goes into planning how the programs will fit together and into organizing testing activity. This book is not about how to write a computer program but how to be part of a team that designs, writes, and tests a whole set of computer programs.

Most new software projects tend to get into trouble, i.e., to get behind schedule or to be over budget. This little book then is for anyone who expects to be involved with software development and has had little exposure to it. It is meant to demystify software engineering activities. You don't even need to be able to read a computer program to understand this book, but by the time you have finished reading it you should have an improved grasp of what to expect. Whether you are a high-level manager, an engineering supervisor, or an entry-level programmer, you will discover that software development is becoming an engineering discipline with rules and conditions that should be obeyed.

Software Development, as used here, means the creation of integrated sets of computer programs that satisfy specifications. The functions that are performed usually require many separate programs which work together. Everything gets complicated very quickly, and the software developer *must* understand what is going on at his/her working level. The tendency toward runaway complexity in software design has led to ways of controlling the design steps. Such an organized approach requires adequate record keeping; much of the work is planning, analyzing, and writing. An often-quoted industry standard is "60 percent of the effort in design alone, 40 percent on both coding and testing."

The larger the software project, the more important it is that the formalities of the development cycle be adhered to. Projects that require more than three programmers need this software development discipline. As of this writing, for example, government contracts for software require the *deliverables* (documents, reviews) and procedures to be defined at least in the detail that is specified here. In fact, a highly detailed project management directive is usually supplied by the government's project manager. (This book will only incidentally use the technical terminology of such directives because the intent is to keep things generic and to avoid jargon.)

Software development procedures control the simultaneous work of several programmers on one system. The ideal software team is a *single* programmer who (for a very small project):

- Formulates the specifications
- Understands the engineering completely
- Does all of the design analysis
- Lays out the conceptual system of programs
- Writes the programs
- Tests and integrates the programs

The complex interactions between different programs and data can often be held in one's memory. The actual activities that are the steps in software development are contained there in a latent form. When all the thinking (conscious and unconscious) is done in the same head, tremendous efficiency and coordination are possible. As soon as two or more programmers work in parallel, however, communication requires needed written documentation. Suddenly the development is a team effort, with all of the benefits and problems that are entailed.

Even without a team approach, though, the documentation is needed for the customer and future users. A large software system requires customer approvals at critical times in its development. This guarantees that the desired specifications are being designed into the system. Written records act as a protection for both the customer and the developer. Even for small projects the documents that will be discussed throughout this text are needed in simple form for orderly activity.

These development rules evolved from necessity. Customers had to know what they were buying. In a big project the vendor had to know the product under design was an acceptable one. An out-of-control development is a businessman's nightmare. The project gets seriously behind schedule and before long is likely to operate in the red. The field is full of horror stories of software developers who have "lost their shirts." Had the rules set forth here been followed, problems and pitfalls could have been avoided, saving both time and dollars.

Certain types of software development are critically sensitive to planning and scheduling. A fixed-price commitment, for example, is taken very seriously, and many vendors rarely consider it for entirely new software. Projects developing both new hardware and the software to support it can have grave scheduling problems: The hardware *must* be finished first in order to test the software, or expensive simulators have to be designed and built.

Since the art of software development is still in the process of becoming standard engineering practice, the rules are still changing. An increasing number of papers on the subject are appearing in the programming literature. What is presented in this book is a snapshot of typical development practices as used recently by most large companies.

The term management was deliberately avoided in the title because no actual management methods or techniques (common to general applications) are discussed. The only topics that are covered are those procedures and products unique to software development. Where appropriate, references to details and sophisticated methodology are provided. This book is meant to be simple and brief so that the subject is of manageable size. Such an approach is cheerfully modeled after Kernighan and Plauger's excellent *Elements of Programming Style*[1], as they applied Strunk and White's *Elements of Style*[2], in the attempt to tame a forbidding subject.

Software development activity is covered from two points of view. Chapters 1 to 16 are descriptive of the environment in a software project and of the documents that are written in support of the project. The message is clear that software development produces mostly paper—and this according to formal guidelines. The remainder of the book describes the activity of software development, putting all of the documentation that has been discussed into context.

Actual parts of the Department of Defense Automated Data Systems Documentation Standards (DoD Standard 7935.1S, September 1977) are included as appendixes. These are prescribed tables of contents for several of the important engineering and design documents. They are much more detailed and rigorous than what is covered in this book but give the flavor of what is expected for some Defense Department software development.

Finally, a brief epilogue mentions other less conventional approaches to software development and the reasons why people tried them.

NOTES

1. B. W. Kernighan and P. J. Plauger, *The Elements of Programming Style* (New York: Yourdon, 1974).

2. W. Strunk Jr. and E. B. White, *The Elements of Style* (New York: MacMillan, 1959).

Confronting a New Software Project

The Big Questions 1

A software project really begins when you write the proposal for it. The proposal requires a demonstration of expertise, which will be shown naturally if the author has a clear idea of:

- What is to be done
- What his resources are for doing it
- How it will be done and scheduled

By the time a convincing proposal has been written, company management has already begun to confront the project. Most good proposals even suggest names of the qualified staff members who will probably be assigned. A schedule and cost estimate are nearly always included, and a preliminary design is at least suggested. The potential project is already part of the company's agenda.

At contract award, the sudden new drain on resources should already be planned for. The author of the proposal should have already thought a lot about the design and the requirements to be satisfied. Sources of long lead-time items should already have been identified. In short, the proposal preparation automatically includes a lot of project preparation. The preparation of the proposal is a test of the competence of the staff to understand the requirements and to begin the design.

There have been companies who avoided assigning proposal writers to the project. In this case, most of the above benefits of the proposal are lost because:

- The project personnel may be totally unfamiliar with the requirements.
- Most likely they have not thought much about the project in advance.
- They have *not* been tested, as to relevant competence, by preparing the proposal.
- There is no "line of continuity" of responsibility maintained from proposal through inception of work.
- A lot of useful start-up information that wasn't written into the proposal will probably be lost.

With these conditions the project begins "under a cloud"; starting up is certainly more painful and probably very disorganized, and the operation may be in trouble from the start.

A PROJECT EXAMPLE

We need an example of a typical software project that we can follow throughout the book. There is no typical software project any more (it used to be business data processing). We have chosen the timely example of an energy-generating network simulation. (This is a fictitious example developed primarily for use by the author.) The Request for Proposal (RFP) asks for a computer program that imitates the behavior of a large number of small power-generating systems based on alternative forms of energy, i.e.:

- Windmills
- Small solar generators
- Cogenerators (companies generating power from their waste heat, feeding excess to the line)
- Tidal-action generators

The program is to simulate the way in which all of these different generators interact with the power grid of existing utilities.

Consider, for example, 25 small solar plants, 75 windmills, 5 tidal-action generators, and 250 cogenerators located all over California. Each of these plants will develop power that varies with location, time of day, time of year, weather, and other conditions. The Alternative Energy Agency wants to be able to predict the effect these generators will have on available power everywhere in California, so they can plan the generator's locations and sizes to do the most good. The system is too big and too complicated for simple calculations to be useful, so a computer model is needed that tests different types, locations, sizes, and numbers. This example is as "typical" as anything else of current big software "packages." This kind of system is familiar, it is easy to visualize what is being "imitated" in the program, and it is complicated enough to resemble reality.

The lucky firm that won this contract is typical of the hundreds of small energy-oriented firms which exist because of the energy crisis. Far-Out Energy Systems, Inc., has engineered portions of advanced solar and wind power systems, has done extensive consulting on cogeneration, and has performed several large studies for the Alternative Energy Agency. Until now, however, their four-person software team has only created software to support analysis for large studies, but the fifteen other technical staff members are sharp engineer-scientists who are familiar with computer modeling and knowledgeable of generating systems. They wrote a good proposal because they understood:

- What was intended
- How the system worked

- What software would be needed
- What a realistic schedule would be

At contract award they are suddenly *on* this schedule in the proposal, and it will be the driving force that determines assignments and activities. The pattern of what will be done is the Statement of Work that the proposal promised to carry out. This has been condensed and is shown below (in actuality it contained fifteen pages of details).

Now that the contract work has begun, the contractor plans the course of the entire project. Three important steps must now be followed:

1. Finding what resources are needed and what are on hand
2. Verifying that the shedule in the proposal is realistic
3. Producing the plans and documents that show what will be produced and the guidelines for producing it

With efforts now under way to achieve these points, the development work has begun. The following chapters will elaborate on these preparatory steps and will describe the development process.

STATEMENT OF WORK

1.0 General Requirements
The contractor will furnish a computer simulation of the network functioning of small electric power generating stations feeding power into the main public utility grid.

1.1 This computer program will simulate the effect of these generators upon available electric power everywhere in the network's area.

1.2 This computer program will allow the major power output characteristics of the following types of generator to be modeled:
- Solar cells
- Windmill
- Waste-burning steam
- Solar turbine
- Tidal

2.0 This computer program will be capable of execution on at least three major vendors' computer systems that are large enough to handle the model's size and that differ only in mass-storage input-output language.

3.0 Power generator parameters to be modeled: The computer simulation program will take into account the following variations of output due to the nature of the generator or its location:
- Time of year
- Geographic location
- Availability of fuels
- Time of day
- Weather
- Generator condition

4.0 The computer model will be capable of simulating in one system:
- 5,000 solar cell generators
- 500 windmills
- 100 solar turbines
- 1,000 tidal generators
- 1,000 waste-burning steam generators

5.0 The simulation model will be capable of modeling two years of model time (of the maximum size) in less than five hours of real-time computation.

6.0 All the data supporting the computation will be loaded in a supporting data base prior to the computation.

7.0 As the computation proceeds, the currently available results will be available in mass-storage files for on-line examination and analysis.

8.0 The computer system used will support interactive, on-line data entry, data analysis, and software maintenance and batch execution of the simulation with hard-copy output upon demand.

9.0 The simulation will be operable by staff who are not professionally trained programmers or software engineers.

Resources Needed

People   2

It is the people who make it all happen. Creativity has real meaning in the software industry, and creative people are sought and usually are rewarded. Only in the fine arts is the individual's worth more obvious. Not only is the high achiever a fantastic producer of software, but his abilities propagate to others in various ways. The super designer or super programmer can make a mediocre crew do great things, if given the chance. Such a person can:

- Teach others how to use the available software tools
- Provide on-the-job training while supervising the actual work
- Ensure that the software design is really good and instruct the programmers in how it works
- Inspire others with the example of high achievement and an enthusiastic approach

It is a lucky firm that has one such person for every ten other people. It is a wise firm that knows his value.

The most neglected value is training. Even experienced professionals usually need additional instruction to produce special software. Part of resource assessment in the power plant simulation example consists of planning a small training program on the computer simulation. It remains true that the best programmer has a good grasp of what the program is really supposed to do, and the software staff needs engineering instruction in the functions of the small power generator network and in the models for each type of generator. The engineering staff also needs instructions in preparing design specifications that can be understood by programmers. Far-Out Energy Systems acted with foresight in scheduling directly into the proposal the hours needed for training.

Since the company plans to hire two additional programmers who will also need instruction, their training will last well into the duration of the project. Here is where the possibility of trouble occurs: When the project begins to get behind schedule (as many software projects do), there is an overwhelming temptation to cut training so more work will get done. Don't do it! The most productive use of expert staff is the training they give to others, at least part-time. The use of 100 percent of an expert's time to write programs has been described as "Eating your seed corn!"

One of the problems with software staffing is that almost everyone has to be an expert of some kind. Individuals are not very interchangeable, as these necessary software specializations show:

- Managers familiar with engineering and software
- Engineers who understand the hardware or system being modeled
- Engineers-designers who can translate engineering specifications into descriptions of data and the processes software can perform
- Programmers who understand enough engineering to participate in the early design of software functions
- Programmers who simply write code from detailed software and data descriptions and can debug programs
- Technical specialists who can:
  —Formulate procedures and standards
  —Administer software record keeping
  —Administer schedule management
  —Promote quality assurance (QA)
  —Test and certify software
- Support people
  —Secretaries
  —Typists
  —Reproduction machine operators
  —Data-entry personnel
  —Computer operators

It is hard to find many of these specialists who have adequate experience. This is probably because the software industry is expanding rapidly, and the pool of trained people is always smaller than the demand (another reason why a permanent training program is almost always necessary). The competition for experienced people is so fierce that personnel turnover in purely technical software firms can reach 30 percent (per year) and is usually at least 20 percent. This has a profound effect on the course of a typical software project! The project will almost certainly lose some of its key people long before it is finished. Project planning must include how to immediately replace key people without wrecking other projects the company is working on. Without overstaffing, the only obvious way to do this is to "break in" another person for each key job while the project progresses. This understudy would, of course, spend the major portion of time at his/her own job.

The software industry suffers badly from the effects of job turnover. It is almost impossible to protect a project from the loss of key people, because they are the ones everyone is trying to hire. Consultant firms point out that the cost in time spent breaking in a new person on specialized work may average six months of his labor (it takes that long to understand some software enough to become productive). The arithmetic is depressing. Consider that you have to replace 20 out of 100 people per year (a turnover of 20 percent) and that their direct labor averages $50,000 each per year. Add to this recruitment cost of about $10,000 per replacement, and a firm can spend some $700,000 for these 20 employees. This is a lot of staff overhead for a little firm of 100 people to carry, and it helps to explain why software is so expensive.

This replacement cost rarely shows up as a clear-cut accountable item because no one can agree on how long it takes for a new employee to become productive. Even if the break-in period were only one month, our turnover cost would be over $100,000 for twenty replacements! It is no wonder so many innovative schemes are being tried to keep workers happy and to get more "bang per buck" out of labor costs by reducing turnover. Magazine and newspaper articles have appeared for years on menu benefit plans, properly designed bonuses for longevity or productivity, at-work recreational facilities, etc. When turnover costs this much, you have a big pool of "lost dollars" to tap to correct the problem. Enhanced awareness of good human relations with employees will certainly encourage them to stay. Good software people are highly trained and individualistic with a great deal of self-respect; praise for good work and consideration for their opinions are essential to them.[1] They feel that they know what they are doing and how to do it and hence are more critical of management than other technical people. People who change jobs are just as likely to do it because of their disillusionment with management as they are for more money.

Project continuity of personnel is one of the major headaches in the software industry. It has emphasized the role of good written supporting material in cases where no one is left who understands how the software works. This is one of the reasons that so much effort must go into written text in the development process.

NOTES

1. This subject is covered in detail in Gerald M. Weinberg, *The Psychology of Computer Programming* (New York: Van Nostrand-Reinhold, 1971).

Writing and Publishing Capabilities   3

Most software companies are in the publishing business, whether they realize it or not. IBM is the world's second largest publisher after the U.S. government. Every software project implies a heavy commitment to writing, editing, and publishing (which is why most of this book is about software documents). Much of this documentation can be produced by people not engaged in the design or coding activities, thus freeing the technical specialists for their specialties. Any large engineering firm automatically has a technical publications department. If the company produces software it has more work than for hardware engineering.

In our example company, Far-Out Energy Systems, they had expected to add two typists when the big simulation project came in. They are surprised by the heavy graphics and typing load when people start to write documents. It soon becomes necessary to contract out some artwork, and they consider hiring a full-time technical editor (instead of their part-time one).

As soon as the software writing starts to flow, the load on the copier soars. It is seldom realized how much interengineer communication depends on circulating copies. Software makes particularly large demands on everyone knowing what everyone else is doing. The number of copies made goes up as the square or the cube of the number of people on the project. The copying machine can almost stop a big project dead in its tracks by breaking down at the wrong time. It is particularly important that copying be available as a service by publications staff, so expensive specialists aren't used for mass-production copying. However, software people usually like to be able to run small numbers of copies themselves for their immediate colleagues, so most firms now provide do-it-yourself copiers as well.

Dictation of text (instead of scribbling) has long been proven to be worth the cost of the equipment in terms of increased productivity. Vendors sometimes sell classes in dictation technique, either live on the premises or as cassettes. As word processors become cheaper they are proving to offer an even larger increase in output than any previous technical gadget. Many newspapers now have them for their reporters, and for a writer who can type, nothing else provides such speed and built-in editing capability.

For software writing the text editor on the computer used in the development frequently serves well as a word processor. (A text editor usually implies a terminal communicating directly with the computer.) However, it shouldn't be allowed to tie up terminals needed for design or coding. Sometimes it can be arranged for the word processor computer to communicate (in both directions) with the larger development computer. This is a convenience for designers who may be using machine-resident programs to analyze or format design text or pictures. In recent years the medium for expressing a design has begun changing from flow charts (pictures) to *program design language* (PDL) (formatted text). PDL processors and formatters are only resident on "real" computers, so communication between the main computer and the staff's word processor has become even more important to make text movable.

The load on publication facilities increases almost exponentially with the size of the project. For a project staff of five people or less, the documentation can be absorbed in an average department's work load without strain. When a software project grows to fifteen people or larger, the necessary detail in documents requires far more person-hours dedicated to the technical effort. At this point the person-hours writing and editing documents becomes comparable to the effort spent analyzing, designing, coding, and testing.

Computer Hardware and Terminals

4

Few software projects are allowed the luxury of choosing their computer. The central processing unit (*mainframe*) and magnetic storage units (disk memory and/or tape drives) are usually specified by the customer. In most cases the nature of the project is the basis for the selection, or the customer might already own the computer. The software developer must have people who can work with whatever computer system the project calls for. Usually some of the staff require training to be productive. The developer should, however, be aware of computer hardware supporting units (*peripherals*) that allow effective use of the computer for development. These devices are terminals, printers, graphic-display devices, and plotters.

The days of IBM cards and programming with only line printer print-outs are past, and a good thing, too! Today, every self-respecting programmer expects to be able to spend half his working day at a terminal if necessary. Almost all coding, debugging, and testing should be done by someone at a terminal. With the software design aids available now, most documentation and design can be done far more effectively at a terminal than at a desk. The best combination for a software team is to have at least one display screen-type terminal for every two software people. There should also be several high-speed printing terminals or one fast line printer for the project (or more, for a project of greater than twenty software people). These devices should all access the computer at once in a fast-response time-sharing mode. The consequence of too few terminals is lowered productivity. Software people are now so well paid that money is saved by buying enough terminals.

Graphic-display terminals are substantially more expensive than those that are limited to printing, but their need is usually prescribed by the project. The same is true for computer-driven plotting devices.

In our example company, even though the computer was not named by the customer, it was understood from private hints. Far-Out Energy Systems felt they needed one graphic-display terminal to show their simulated power grid and parameters on a map. Since six software people would be at work at once, they bought two more display screen terminals (CRTs) in addition to the one they had, and they also rented a high-speed line printer and communication device for the project duration (on a lease-purchase plan so the rent would apply if they decided to buy it later). The computer itself is a large commercial time-sharing system providing nationwide service. The intended operation of these terminals is that hard copy will be obtainable immediately by a programmer simply by typing the request into a terminal.

CRTs are generally regarded as more convenient for programming and design chores; word processors use them almost exclusively. Unless the terminals are in the same building as the computer, each one must be equipped with a communications device (modem) that adapts it to a telephone. Large installations use a single massive communications computer without telephones to service the line printer, the card reader, and all terminals together.

Along with the computer hardware a complete set of user manuals should be provided for every programmer. Even experienced programmers cannot get along without consulting manuals to resolve tricky questions about programming languages, data definitions, and control instructions for the hardware. Every staff should have at least one expert who can function as a consultant on the fine points of computer operation. It is occasionally discovered that the computer or its languages don't work exactly as the manufacturer claimed they would. Such system bugs shouldn't be allowed to impede progress any longer than necessary, and a specific expertise should be available to avoid this.

Automated Development Aids   5

Programmers need all the help they can get from their computer. They can get it from programs which are resident on the computer memory and which convert the programmer's text into software products. All such programs that aid the programmer are called *development aids* or, taken as a group, the *Software Development Environment* (SDE).

A programmer of very early computers had no such help. The instructions contained in the programs were just long numbers (*machine language*) that told the computer what actions to perform. Program ming was arduous and slow, and the machine was terribly unhelpful. We have come a long way from that. First, programming languages were developed so that words (or at least letters) could be used in computer instructions. These languages evolved into those that could be learned easily (e.g., BASIC). Now there are both general-purpose languages (e.g., FORTRAN) and special-purpose languages (e.g., SIMSCRIPT for simulation).

In recent years improvements in languages have been devoted to making programs more easily understood. The idea of *structured programming* (easily readable programs) led to languages that inherently streamline the logic of a program so it is easier to read.

There was a period of several years during which language improvements were the programmer's only new aids. When text editors appeared the computer could be used as a word processor for programs, data, and anything else that had to be entered into the system to support the software. A text editor usually implies a terminal communicating directly with the computer. This interactive capability is one of the greatest aids a programmer has. Without the ability to enter and execute programs (at least for debugging) interactively, the programmer is living in the "Dark Ages" of software. This is why there should be at least one terminal for every two programmers; the programmer can then spend at least half of the work day actually improving his programs. Typically, 80 percent of this time will be spent using the text editor to enter or edit all of the text that the software requires. The better the text editor, the more effective the programmer.

Nothing new is perfect—especially a new computer program. Getting the bugs out of a program usually takes at least three times as long as writing it. In addition to the language improvements that were made, features evolved for showing what went on in an executing program. These debugging aids, still in the mainstream of development for most languages, are facilities which make it easier for a programmer to display values of data items during actual execution and which are associated with the program failing. Each computer vendor has his own version of these aids, and there are software firms that specialize in them.

Programs are permeated by their data and structured by their control logic. Almost the entire structure of a program is determined by the:

- Data used for control
- Data entered as input
- Data produced as output
- Control logic that determines processing

The logical structures for all of these data have to be defined in advance of a computer program's definition. It is surprising that aids for data definition didn't keep pace with language improvements. For years the one data structure used for almost everything was the long list of names or numbers (*sequential file*). This corresponded to storage on a reel of magnetic tape. The sequential file, a list of sets of data items (*records*), had to be scanned from the beginning to access a desired set of items. When modern disk memories replaced tapes as input to programs, many ways of better organizing data became possible. Computer vendors provided software to handle data definitions so the burden of defining structures was no longer on each program. Along with this software (usually a language of itself), the vendor provided programs that used these data definitions to handle the data. Thus was born the *data management system* (DMS). DMSs now abound for most sizes of computer (even including personal computers) and are also sold by software firms. Like most different ways of doing things, they have their own limitations including:

- Being available for only a few types of computer
- An inability to support "any old program" that wants to use it
- Possibly only allowing certain types of logical data structure
- Being slow to process data, compared with custom-written programs

A new programmer immediately discovers that he must confront the computer through its own program, the *operating system*. This program, which controls what the computer does, has its own *job control language* (JCL). Vendors are very proud of their JCLs, but usually not because they are simple. It is sad, but learning a JCL for a given computer is more arduous than learning FORTRAN. And it's only good for that one type of computer! Usually vendors try to extend all the things that can be done in their JCL, thus adding to its complexity. This ultimately lets the programmer have more power to express himself, but he certainly has earned it! The best compromise is a JCL with a lot of different words in it to let you do different things but with simple punctuation that is easy to remember. Recently some vendors added normal program language logical power and structure (e.g., *IF statements* and *subroutines*) to their JCL, improving the ability to control large systems of programs and their data. A feature even more desirable is the ability to have job control statements as part of programs (rarely available).

Aids to the design of software have appeared in the last few years as programs that:

- Generate hierarchy and data flow charts
- Generate flow charts
- Generate design language descriptions
- Coordinate and cross reference requirements for analysis

Flow charts are the traditional way of depicting program design, so programs that aid in producing them are helpful. Flow charts are being replaced by design languages, which show a written description of a program using English-language phrases. A design language program has keywords that cause indenting of the written text so it looks like a program and has a similar logic structure. It is usually much easier than flow charting:

- To write PDL
- To understand PDL
- To make changes to PDL
- To convert PDL to a program

Figure 5-1 shows a design language description of a program and the matching flow chart. Other major advantages are that design language input can be prepared on the computer's own text editor, similarly to a program or data definition, and cross referencing is produced as output by most design language programs. (Appendix J shows how a PDL can be used to describe software development itself.)

A useful design aid is a program that helps to keep track of specifications and requirements for a software system. This type of aid is only for very large system development and is especially necessary when the software may have 100 requirements to satisfy. Since satisfaction

Flow Chart	Program Design Language

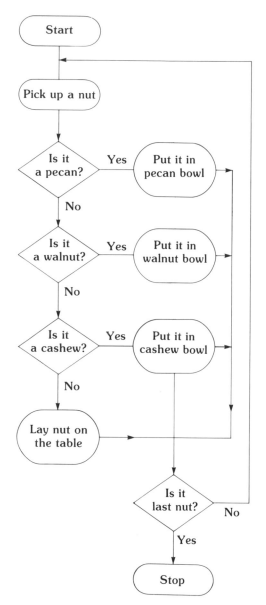

For every nut in a mixed bowl:

    Pick up a nut

        If it is a pecan
           Put it in pecan bowl

        Else if it is a walnut
           Put it in walnut bowl

        Else if it is a cashew
           Put it in cashew bowl

        Else
           Put it on the table

Do next nut, until all separated

Figure 5.1. A flow chart versus program design language

Describe a program to separate a bowl of mixed pecans, walnuts, and cashews into separate bowls for each kind.

of the requirements of software must be testable, a semiautomated way of bookkeeping and cross referencing is very helpful. Such a system, which can be hooked into the design language cross-referencing capability, can also help to automatically generate test cases that otherwise have to be thought out individually. (Requirements software and test management software have currently been developed by a few big software vendors solely for their own use, but they are almost certain to be commercially available soon.)

Far-Out Energy Systems chose the computer system which best pleased their customer, and by using commercial time-sharing they got access to all the usual development aids that fit that computer. They pay a usage rental fee on the PDL processor, which is proprietary software. They chose FORTRAN-77, the latest version of the language, which is standard on most large computers. This satisfies paragraph 2.0 of the Statement of Work (see page 3), which requires the simulation program to work on three major vendors' systems, except for input/output (I/O) statements. The exclusion of I/O statements from the requirements also allows them to use the vendor's data definition and access language to simplify data design and references in programs. Far-Out Energy knows of no special debugging software that is available, but as the project progresses they may find one. Their project doesn't appear to justify any automation of requirements analysis or test generation.

The Products of
Software
Development

The Standards and Conventions Guide   6

It can sometimes be difficult to distinguish between a standard and a convention, but, in general, most standards and conventions are simply specifications on the content of documents or programs, relating where they will be located and how they should appear.

Any product of quality meets certain standards. The *standards* of software excellence, which are still evolving, affect both the form and the content of the programs, data, and documents. *Conventions*, on the other hand, are more local: they depend on design approach and general concurrence about how designing, coding, and writing should be done.

Standards have the most profound effect on the software design. An example might be that the principles as outlined in this book are to be followed in a project. In such a case, relevant portions of this book would be incorporated into the Standards and Conventions Guide (and also other software documents such as the development plan).

Another primary standard might be that design must be completed before the programs are written. (Don't laugh—it happens the other way too often!) Other generally accepted standards are that structured design and programming will be used or that programs will be *modular* with only one function to each program. (This will be discussed further in Chapter 13 on design.)

Conventions include such practices as programs being no longer than two pages or not indenting decimal-numbered paragraphs in documents.

Current fashions in programming have a big effect on what conventions and standards are adopted for both design and coding. Small software projects (four people or less) may have very brief Standards and Conventions Guides, while large projects can have a book that is more than a quarter-inch thick. The coordinating effect of standards and conventions upon complex activities thus becomes apparent, determining the communication formalities between the project staff, as well as how to do designing, coding, and writing.

The setting of standards and conventions should not cause lots of extra work, merely clarity, neatness, and predictability. The following points should be covered if possible:

- What is the programming language? What available features in the language should be avoided where this is not too difficult?
- What should the programs contain (e.g., comments describing all variables, what the program does, and its relation to other programs as well as declarations of all variable types)?
- What should be the format of the program listings (e.g., where the descriptive comments should be put, where the variables should be declared, where the communication variables should be described)?
- What medium is required to express the design, i.e., flow charts or design language?
- What points must be covered in the design such as I/O data descriptions, interprogram communication, methods of processing?
- What principles are to be followed in the design of data structures and programs? These can range from general principles such as structured programming to details such as how programs communicate with each other and how they are controlled.
- What should be the format of design documents (i.e., where should data definitions go, where should processing be described, etc.)?
- What conventions should be followed in creating names for data items and programs? It is critical that a convention be chosen early to aid in categorizing things. Names should be structured so that their hierarchical relationships (who "owns" whom) are built into them where possible. This can lead to names that are automatically generated in a text editor or by an editing program. It assures more understandability in the software. A compressed example of a Standards and Conventions Document is given on page 27; it shows a tried-and-true naming convention.
- A glossary of technical terms (using standard meanings) should be developed before design begins and probably should be among the standards and conventions. This glossary is critical, especially in projects with highly specialized hardware. Engineers frequently refer to one item with several different names, and this can lead to absolute chaos among the software designers. An extension of a standard glossary is to make data and program names at least partial mnemonics (suggestive abbreviations) for those things they represent.

The project at Far-Out Energy Systems is not very large, so it is possible for them to organize their Standards and Conventions Guide into a small format. The paragraphs marked with an asterisk (*) are those that should govern *any* project no matter how small; some standards and conventions should always be applied.

STANDARDS AND CONVENTIONS

1.0 The design approach will be based on *top-down* analysis (structured design) with all software functions modular.

2.0 The data structures will be modular in function and centrally defined to avoid duplication of data.

3.0 The design will be expressed as design language for programs and data and also as data flow charts for preliminary design.

*4.0 Requirements and specifications will be expressed as English text, and the first expression of general design criteria will be as English text.

*5.0 Functions performed by the software will be described with respect to their:
    5.1 Input data
    5.2 Output data
    5.3 Intermediate data
    5.4 Processing
    5.5 Control data
    5.6 Hierarchy (HIPO)

6.0 Sets of programs that communicate with each other will reference common data structures.

7.0 Control data for programs will be accepted and processed, wherever possible, prior to execution of any application programs.

*8.0 Programs will contain descriptive headings that mention:
    8.1 What programs use this subprogram
    8.2 What subprograms does this program use
    8.3 Names and purpose of input data
    8.4 Names and purpose of output data
    8.5 Names and purpose of intermediate data
    8.6 What processing is performed in this program

*9.0 All data definitions will include:
    9.1 Name of the data structure
    9.2 Type of data structure (e.g., array, table, item)
    9.3 Kind of datum (e.g., integer, real number, character)
    9.4 Allowable range of values
    9.5 Function performed in the software, i.e., its meaning
    9.6 What programs reference it

10.0 The programming language will be FORTRAN-77.

11.0 The programs will be modular (i.e., each program performs only one function) and hierarchical (i.e., programs will perform subfunctions by calling other programs).

12.0 The principles of structured programming will be followed as long as this doesn't lead to awkward code or seriously slow processing.

13.0 Program listings will be formatted by indention of lines within loops and IF statements.

14.0 English prose description of the program and its data will appear, as comments, at the top of the program underneath the program name.

15.0 Glossary of terms
(Several pages of technical definitions that *must* be used in design descriptions would follow here.)

16.0 The convention to be used for naming data structures is:

16.1 File names will be three characters only, unless four is absolutely needed to avoid ambiguity or to avoid computer-reserved words.

16.2 Data structures within a file will begin with the first three characters of the file name.

17.0 Program names will begin with the first three characters of the major subsystem name (the top-level program that is referenced by the executive system).

18.0 Programs used for general-purpose functions will be considered to belong to the utility subsystem and be so named.

The Development Schedule 7

The schedule usually dominates everything. Completion of the work on schedule is the first criterion of success measured by both customers and management. More Golden Rules of correct practice are violated in the name of the schedule than for any other reason. If this is the case, it means that unforeseen things impeded development or that the schedule was inherently unrealistic. It is a truth of history that many software projects aren't completed on schedule, even though the schedule is considered law. The most important thing a software manager or leader does is to devise a schedule that can be met.

As mentioned earlier, in most cases the schedule is already decided when the proposal is submitted. The resource evaluation and preliminary design completed during the proposal preparation are the basis for this schedule. If the software is all new, with the design only fuzzily understood, then a lot of research is involved in the development. This makes the schedule tentative, based mostly on guesses about the work that will be required to think out new problems. Such guesses are almost *always* optimistic, and if so, the schedule will be a failure. Further, all the sales pressures in bidding on a project promote optimistic schedules. The engineer who admits he doesn't know enough about the design and wants contingency time in the schedule is a "sour-puss." Adequate time for training people new to the project is also often underestimated, but the crowning difficulty is protecting the schedule against the departures of key people.

The chances are in favor of the schedule being so tight that the project cuts corners on intended good practices. The creation of an achievable schedule requires knowledge of the software's complexity and familiarity with the staff's abilities. There is *no* substitute for experience with both of these. The manager-engineer who devises the schedule must have calibrated the project against the past performances of his/her own (or someone else's) people. A contract which takes account of changed requirements and which can extend the schedule is essential. Cost estimation programs are available that assist in schedule, as well as cost, estimation. They all require, however, that previous performance on similar software be known. It is essential that the basis for schedule estimation include both time for good documentation and effective management practices.

One such scheduling practice is the critical path method (CPM) of controlling bottlenecks (critical paths). This is based on the idea that "You have to finish 'this' before you start 'that,' " where this and that are tasks in the project. Such related tasks must be identified before the work actually starts and completion times assigned for tasks that need to be accomplished first. There are semiautomated computer aids that produce charts showing these critical paths in schedules. The difficulty is in finding someone to collect the data for this charting after the schedule starts to get tight, but this is when CPM scheduling is needed most. It is important to recognize which tasks must be finished first when other tasks depend on their results. Another good scheduling practice is to give people stable assignments in the project, not splitting time among several tasks. For most people the loss of momentum in switching subject matter leads to inefficiency and poor morale, yet this principle is almost always violated when the schedule starts to slip.

The most insidious "corner cut" to "save time" is the cessation of training to free people to do the work. This most often results in such low productivity that the schedule is worse off than before. In large organizations there is a tendency to suddenly add extra new people to the staff to save a schedule. This method, called the "Chinese Army Approach," is almost always done at the last minute as an act of desperation. The theory is that ten people can finish the work of one person in one tenth the time. The actuality is that now most of the effort of the original crew is spent training the new people to be productive. Sensible working-level project leaders refuse extra help at the last minute, unless the help is already totally familiar with the task.[1]

The main effect of a schedule slippage is to downgrade excellence. There is not the time to do it right, but it is always thought that there is time to do it over. If the software is to be rigorously tested and the requirements are detailed and complete, it will be hard to cut corners on performance adequacy. Software that doesn't work properly is usually not salable. The products of software development include many things, however, that can be briefly treated (i.e., most of the documentation), and if a schedule slips early enough to affect the design documents and the cuts are made there, it may not be possible to write code that works properly.

In one project in which the design effort was skimped on to accelerate the schedule, the first attempt at coding failed miserably, and the project ended one-and-a-half years behind schedule! Some documents are essential to understanding the code that is being written, and without these it may not be possible to continue developing existing code. One such example was assembly language code without adequate comments and description that was developed on a fixed-price contract. This project ended two years behind schedule and cost the vendor two million dollars because they had to throw away the assembly language code when too many people left the project (no one remaining could understand the software). It was begun over again in FORTRAN, using mostly contract programmers.

Adequate descriptive documents and heavily commented code are important for all software, but they are absolutely crucial for assembly language or for software that drives exotic hardware.

There are several kinds of software projects in which schedules are almost impossible to correctly estimate, and in such cases fixed-price, fixed-delivery-date contracts are dangerous. Sensible vendors would never think of accepting such conditions. "All new" software projects are an example. The job performed by the programs has not been designed before by the staff of the project, and the design has to be worked out from the ground up as a form of research. Unforeseen problems are continually occurring in research, and the managers would need a crystal ball to predict the contingencies in such a project. It is just as bad if the staff has no experience in building software that is of a standard type to the industry. The important point is that the software design is all new to the staff, and the crucial importance of continuing training must be stressed. "An ounce of insight is worth a pound of motivation."

If hardware is being developed in addition to the software to drive it, the possible problems are multiplied by the effect the hardware performance may have on the software (and vice versa). Obviously these effects can't truly be tested until the physical hardware is actually operational. The schedule, however, requires the assumption that the hardware is completed before many crucial tests on the software can be made. Here again is the likelihood of some appalling surprises that actually require design changes for correction. Thus, new software and hardware together should be approached with extreme caution. Some projects blithely assume they can build a hardware simulation program to make early tests on software. For hardware that doesn't exist yet and for which a design may not be complete, building a simulation can be almost impossible and certainly time consuming. Computer simulation programs deserve a complete project in their own right.

Far-Out Energy Systems' project to build a simulation program and the schedule they worked out should be examined. It was based on performing the work listed in the Statement of Work. The resource assumptions were critical. They assumed that they would lose two key people before the project was half over, that they would hire two new programmers early in the project, and that they would replace the two lost with less experienced people late in the project. Much of the preliminary design was contained in the proposal; only this let them feel confident in their schedule estimate, which included time for some training of both new hires and old staff. Critical path analysis of the project was already contained in the proposal. Costs were based on continued inflation in the economy of 12 percent. The individual bars in the chart in Figure 7-1 correspond to the topics described in the Software Development Plan (see Chapter 8).

NOTES

1. F. P. Brooks, Jr. *The Mythical Man-Month* (New York: Yourdon, 1975). Much of this book is devoted to fallacies on the subject.

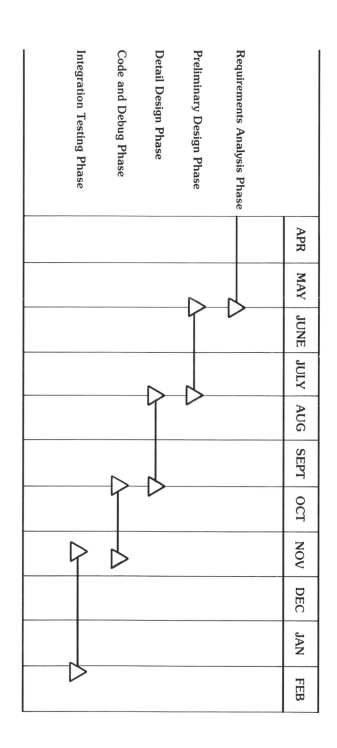

**Figure 7.1. Schedule for Development of
Power Generation Simulator**

The Software Development Plan and the Quality Assurance Plan   8

THE DEVELOPMENT PLAN

The development plan is a detailed guided tour through the development process written for the benefit of the participants. (For a more detailed discussion, refer to the section, The Phases of Software Development.) A major purpose of the plan is to define steps in the development so that they can be checked off and certified when completed. This gives the schedule meaning and provides for step by step approvals, *reviews* or *baselines*, of what has been done by management and customers. For big projects such steps may require several days of presentations on the work that has been performed. Smaller divisions of progress are called *milestones*, and *inchstones* refers to the formal weekly status reporting.

Along with the phases of the development, the plan assigns responsibilities for different phases of the project to the various groups. These assignments say what each group will be doing and how it will know when its work is done. This plan complements the Standards and Conventions Guide by describing the purpose and content of all software documents that are produced as well as the steps for producing these documents. It also establishes administrative procedures for the project. Finally, no good plan ignores contingencies. The development plan prescribes actions that are to be taken by management to solve foreseeable problems. Handling requests for new specifications, for example, should be a clear cut process with both customer and management responsibilities outlined.

The phases of the project that are covered in the development plan and the schedule points that end each phase are:

- System Specification: This involves generation of the Requirements and Specifications Document and culminates in the system review. The schedule, development plan, standards and conventions, and configuration plan are finished for the most part during this phase. Collaboration with the customer is necessary at this point, and the customer *must* approve the specifications produced.

- Systems Analysis: This is a general description of what the software will do. A preliminary design of the system is made that describes a set of functions which satisfy the specifications. The phase culminates in a preliminary design review (or a Functional Design Review).
- Final Software Design: This first involves converting general software functions into descriptions of individual programs. Both data and programs must then be described in enough detail for programmers to know what to code. This phase culminates in what may be called a final design review (or Critical Design Review).
- Design Implementation: This phase includes writing actual computer programs and data definitions and testing them. The debugging and testing is only done of individual programs. The phase culminates in delivery of the software to the Configuration Management Team (the housekeeping group). At this point the test group should do all further testing.
- Testing: This involves testing subsystems and the whole system. The phase certifies that the specifications have been met so that the system can be delivered to the customer. Many customers then do some of their own acceptance testing as well.
- Operational Use: This refers to operational use of the delivered system. This phase requires occasional fixing of undiscovered software failures. This is considered maintenance and goes on as long as the software is used.

The above parts of the software development activity are called the *software life cycle*. (The frontispiece of this book shows the stages of this cycle.)

THE QUALITY ASSURANCE PLAN

There are so many things affecting software quality that a system of "checks" needs to be organized. With software, quality is affected by:

- Standards and conventions for design
- Standards and conventions for coding
- Design methodology (e.g., top-down, structured)
- Adequate satisfaction of requirements
- Testing methodology
- Programming expertise
- Other procedures more related to the management of the above elements

These aspects of development are already prescribed in the various documents and plans. *Quality assurance* (QA) assures that people have performed their jobs in the way they were supposed to. Enforcement is a harsh word, but there have to be established ways of seeing that the guidelines are generally followed. A means of appeal should also exist for cases that the rules don't fit. The ways in which QA is enforced and the means of appealing exceptions are described in the Quality Assurance Plan. It is the guiding document for the Quality Assurance Group, which reports directly to the project manager.

The QA group is the watchdog over activities of most other groups. The plan is devoted to describing what the group will monitor, when they will monitor, how they will monitor, and at what times they are required to certify compliance. For large projects this includes describing a great deal of record keeping. The group's organization is also prescribed in this document.

All activities affecting quality are monitored, and the results are recorded. Those items that are studied are:

- Consistency and clarity of the requirements document
- Correctness and completeness of the requirements cross reference list
- Relevance of the test plan to both of the above
- Whether the functional description is following prescribed design standards
- Format completeness of the functional descriptions and the data flow
- Whether the prescribed design methodology is actually being followed
- Adequacy of detailed design as presented in the design walk-throughs
- Completeness and consistency of the design materials to be presented at the design reviews
- Completeness and consistency of the project documents
- Whether configuration management activities are being carried out as prescribed
- Whether standards and conventions for code, as determined from the structured walkthroughs for each coded module, are being followed
- Adequacy of the unit tests as to format and content of each unit test folder
- Whether integration and test procedures are correctly being followed

- Whether delivery and installation procedures are correctly being followed

This monitoring should take place as soon as there is something to monitor in order to avoid a pile up of chores at critical times. Methods of monitoring will depend on project size and how much paperwork is associated with record keeping.

The Configuration Management Plan

9

Changes to a growing software system must be kept under control. Many individual programs are shared by various parts of the software system. An ill-conceived change can reverberate around the whole software system, upsetting everyone. To prevent this, existing programs and data structures must always be administered carefully. This is done by configuration management (CM), where *configuration* refers to a particular version of the system being assembled—a configuration of programs, data definitions, and data that has a unique identity. Sometimes a large software shop will have in its files a hundred configurations of only a few different systems.

The final design documents are usually the earliest products to come under configuration control. These should include the test plan and its matching list of requirements cross referenced to the design. Once under control, no changes can be made without a list of approvals.

The approval cycle is the heart of CM. It is the tool used to assure that changes raise no unintended problems in the system. This cycle is supported by a lot of paperwork and should also use a computerized information system to handle filing and reporting. This is a beautiful case of software being used to handle its own complexity.

The paperwork covers changes to both the software and all written documents. The following is a listing of various forms and their uses:

- The Problem Report is used to request a change to a program, data definition, or data value. This form could also be called a Software Change Request.
- The Response Report is used to certify that a change to the software has been made. The form should include a description of what was changed and how the change corrected the original problem.
- The Document Update Request is used to request a change to a document or to ask that a new document be provided.
- The Document Update Response is used to certify that a document change request was satisfied. This form usually accompanies the text that satisfies the request.

The changes to the software and documents are not installed as they come in; changes accumulate, however, and are implemented all at once at regular periods, such as weekly. The resulting software update to a new, improved version is called a *build* or is referred to as resulting in a new baseline. This is the way that the "housekeeping" performed by CM lets everyone know the exact status of the software with respect to changes or additions. As new software is added and modifications are made, the older versions are archived (stored) in case something is needed from them.

All of the foregoing activities need to be described in the Configuration Management Plan including the means of storing and retrieving old configurations. Procedures for naming configurations are described that assign the hierarchy of pieces of the software, namely, what belongs to what. These names are used in referring to the software being developed for purposes of scheduling and customer delivery.

If some type of development aid is used to help the software building and storage activities, its use should be prescribed in the plan. Most computer vendors provide such software as an optional feature that works uniquely with their operating system and text editor. Such a program is used to name and create libraries of the programs being developed; it also helps to pull out and modify individual programs that are changed. This is yet another example of software used as a tool to handle the administrative complexities that are inherent in software.

Far-Out Energy Systems was unacquainted with CM when they wrote their proposal. They had never developed software as a product in its own right. Consequently, they had to learn about it from the ground up. They had fortunately planned to have a husky effort devoted to testing and QA, so some of the personnel allocated to these areas were moved over to CM. These reassigned people studied some textbooks on the subject and came up with a plan much too large to include here, but Figures 9-1, 9-2, and 9-3 are examples of their Software Change Requests, Software Response Reports, and Document Change/Response Reports. These forms would be much more complicated for a company that uses more than one type of computer system.

SOFTWARE CHANGE REQUEST

Date: _____
　　　　YY　　　　MM　　　　DD

From: _____

System: _____

Subsystem: _____

Configuration: _____

Request change to: _____

Product ID: _____

Reason change needed:

Suggested change:

Suggested priority: _____

Approvals:

Control no.: _____

Figure 9-1.

SOFTWARE CHANGE RESPONSE

Date: _____
      YY   MM   DD

From: _____

System: _____

Subsystem: _____

Configuration: _____

Control no.: _____

Response to _____ change request

Reason submitted:

Product ID: _____

Change(s) made to:

Description of change(s):

Verification record:

Approvals:

Figure 9-2.

DOCUMENT CHANGE/RESPONSE REPORT

Date: _____
  YY   MM   DD

From: _____

Request or Submit (circle one)

Change to document:

Type: _____

Title: _____

Product ID: _____

Control no.: _____

Response to: _____

Change description:

Change pages (attached):

Verification record:

Approvals:

Figure 9-3.

The Requirements Document

10

Specifications and requirements are the commandments of software development. What will be designed is based on the specifications and requirements; they are the basis of the contract.

The document may be called by different names (such as System Requirement Specification or one of the government terms such as A-Spec) but it always means the same thing. It should be a clear description of what the software must do, including numerical values of capabilities where these are important. It usually takes the form of a list, with each item dealing with only a single requirement. This is so that the requirement may be referenced by paragraph number in all succeeding documents. If a proposal was written, based on a Statement of Work, the Requirements Document is a form of this statement carefully reorganized into a list and edited for clarity.

Specifications and requirements are always stated positively, i.e., what the software *will* do, not what it *will not* do. Requirements must be testable; it must be demonstrated that the software can do whatever is required. The contract to build the software is legally binding, and the vendor must be able to prove the acceptability of the product.

Normally, the list of requirements need not be tightly organized into categories. This is rightly done in the functional design phase of the project. Sometimes different features desired in the software seem to overlap, and this justifiably leads to separate requirement statements with common elements. The completeness of the requirements list is important to the customer because the software need *not* do something unless there is a stated need for it.

Afterthoughts on requirements are expensive (by delaying the project) because software is like a Swiss watch—changing anything can change everything. Modern modular design can minimize this effect, but designers carp bitterly when asked to include late changes in the software. They have a perfect right to complain. The conceptual basis of *any* engineering design is that you decide ahead of time what is going to be built. The foolishness of trying to change a piece of hardware after it is half-built is obvious, and just because computer programs are not machined into steel doesn't make their shape any easier to change. When a software team makes a sincere effort to track a customer's changing ideas by designing as they go, the entire process of design is polluted. Software development is then turned into a service operation. Software is a product, not a service!

The importance of a proposal effort becomes obvious during an analysis of requirements: Most of the work has already been done. A fixed-price bid *must* contain the requirements analysis first; this is what determines the cost of the development. The contract has already been awarded when the official requirements document is begun, implying the vendor has previously estimated cost. This estimate is occasionally too low; project overruns are common in the industry. A software developer who goes over budget on too many projects loses his credibility with potential customers. A developer who misjudges cost on fixed-price contracts loses his shirt.

The requirements list tells everything you have to do, and the schedule states when you have to finish. Together they dominate all activity; as a result, they are worth the effort of the best brains in the project. It is particularly important for the experienced staff members to agree on these two documents. They should not be created by different people than the ones who will do the work.

Far-Out Energy Systems used their Statement of Work (see page 3) as the basis for their Requirements Document. The engineers who did most of the heavy thinking on the proposal were assigned to the tasks of writing the Requirements Document and devising the schedule (which was already suggested in the proposal). Their requirements list is shown below and should be compared with their Statement of Work (see page 3).

(Appendix A is the Department of Defense (DoD) prescribed table of contents for the Requirements Document, or the Functional Description Document. The description of the centrally defined data base requirements is the DoD Data Requirements Document; this table of contents is in Appendix B.)

REQUIREMENTS LIST

1.0 General Requirements
The software system will be a computer simulation of the real-world operation of small electric generators adding power to an established power grid.

  1.1 The software system will be capable of execution on three major makes of computer that are large enough, except for their mass-storage input/output statements, but may require revision between computers.

  1.2 The computation will be data base-driven; i.e., all the data supporting the computation will be loaded in the supporting data base prior to the computation. This will not include all processing control data.

  1.3 The results data will be accessible during the computation in mass-storage files that can be examined and analyzed without interfering with the computation.

  1.4 The simulation system will support both interactive (on-line) and batch operation for:
    1.4.1 Software implementation and maintenance
    1.4.2 Data analysis
    1.4.3 Data entry
    1.4.4 Data display and report generation

1.5 Operation of the simulator will not require:
    1.5.1 Ability to read or modify the programs
    1.5.2 Ability to read or modify data definitions used exclusively by the programs

1.6 All data used to support the model will be specifiable in terms of one of the following:
    1.61 Model structure description
    1.62 Model function description
    1.63 Model results and reporting description
    1.64 Control parameters to operate the simulation

1.7 Failure of the software system to function normally will produce diagnostics specifically related to input, output, or control data; these can be interpreted without reference to actual computer program code.

1.8 Data referenced in more than one part of the software system will be centrally defined and stored (not redundant).

1.9 All data under control of the user will be described in detail in a single data description document that includes:
    1.9.1 All features referenced in Section 1.6
    1.9.2 All features related to use by programs

2.0 Requirements of the Model Simulation

2.1 The computer simulation will quantitatively produce the effect of added available power in a utilities power grid because of a set of small generators added to the grid.

2.2 The following types of small generators will have their characteristics simulated:
    2.2.1 Solar cells
    2.2.2 Solar turbines
    2.2.3 Windmills
    2.2.4 Waste-burning steam
    2.2.5 Tidal

2.3 The following characteristics of the small generators will be modeled:
    2.3.1 Peak-power output
    2.3.2 Wave shapes of voltage and current
    2.3.3 Time variations due to:
        • Time of day
        • Time of year
    2.3.4 Variations of peak output due to:
        • Geographic location
        • Weather
        • Generator condition
        • Availability of fuels

2.4 The size of the computer model will accommodate in one model:
    2.4.1 5,000 solar cell generators
    2.4.2 1,000 waste-burning steam generators
    2.4.3 500 windmills
    2.4.4 100 solar turbines
    2.4.5 1,000 tidal generators

2.5 The speed of computer simulation will be capable of modeling two years of the maximum-size model in less than five hours of elapsed real time.

The Functional Descriptions

11

In order to build something, you first must understand it. For machinery and software you must at least understand what pieces are needed and how they fit together.

The analogy between machinery and software design can be carried pretty far. A machine may have several functions, which are usually related. The more functions there are, the more complex the machine. The initial description of a machine tells what it should do—its functions; individual pieces of a machine may serve more than one function.

So it is with software. The entire software system must perform a collection of related functions. The initial description must be in terms of these functions, and that is the first step in preliminary design.

The actual activity of functional design will be covered later (see Chapter 18), but the list of functions is of concern here. Each function must meet several criteria:

- It must be related to the satisfaction of a requirement (later a cross reference chart will be made).
- It should not overlap with some other function; the whole idea of the design is to separate functions.
- If the function is described in a general way, it should be broken up into more detailed subfunctions.
- It should be stated without explicit reference to any details of computer programs or data. Such details will be covered after all the functions are defined.

All the functions taken as a whole must satisfy all the requirements. A functional analysis is successful if it is complete and contributes some insight into what the software must do. The main purpose of the completed analysis is to remove ambiguities; the secondary purpose is to suggest the structure of the software. That is why functions are hierarchical in nature; that is, a general function is supported by subfunctions, those by sub-subfunctions, etc. The software, as with the functions of the design, should have a hierarchical structure, with programs using subroutines, which in turn use subroutines, etc. Thus, the *functional analysis* begins the process of visualizing the software's structure.

The project at Far-Out Energy Systems yields too large a functional analysis to include here, but a few sample functions were chosen from it and are shown in on page 51. Bear in mind that a functional analysis is not unique, and this is merely one possible way of defining the software's functions.

(The DoD document containing the hierarchical function definitions is The System/Subsystem Specification, whose contents are shown in Appendix C.)

SAMPLE FUNCTIONS OF THE COMPUTER SIMULATOR

1.0 Control Subsystem

    1.1 Log-on and Process Initiator
    This will include entry to the computer and contact with the software controlling a user's access to the simulation programs. The user executes a program that allows choice of how the simulator is to run, and initial control data are entered.

    1.2 Detail Process Control
    This will include entry of the data that prescribe in all necessary detail just what the simulator will do in terms of:
    1.2.1 Mode of control: interactive or batch
    1.2.2 Mode of reporting: during simulation, afterward, or both
    1.2.3 Execution paths through the simulation
    1.2.4 Parameters that vary the conditions under which the simulation operates
    1.2.5 Statistical analysis to be run on the results
    1.2.6 What final reports are desired

    1.3 Error Processing and Responses
    This will include the system's responses to malfunctions in the simulation processing that are due to:
    1.3.1 Incompatible data describing the functions being modeled
    1.3.2 Incompatible specifications for the structure of the model
    1.3.3 Results data produced outside allowable bounds
    1.3.4 Incorrect software behavior
    1.3.5 Incorrect hardware behavior

2.0 Data Management Subsystem

    2.1 Data entry and modification
    This will include all control of the user's access to the data base and the operation of the software that handles data entry and update.
    2.1.1 Data entry: All functions that enter new data
    2.1.2 Data modification: All functions changing old data

    2.2 Data base display and reporting
    This will include all capabilities to display data that are not specifically results of an execution of the simulation program.

3.0 Model-Structuring Subsystem
This will include all software functions that convert user-entered model description data into internal model data which describe the structure of the model to the simulation software. Structure parameters, such as number of small generators versus type and location, existing power pattern in the power grid, etc., are processed by this function.

4.0 Model Operating Subsystem
This will include all software functions that convert user-entered model performance data into simulation parameters of the model for use by the software. Operational descriptive parameters, such as power versus time, fuel, location, weather, etc., are handled by this function.

The sample functions given on page 51 are not as detailed as those most frequently found in a functional analysis. In such a case every paragraph would fill one or two pages with descriptions of subfunctions. The important thing to remember is that functions strongly suggest computer programs and their subroutines and data. The next stage of design will then flow smoothly out of the one before.

The Requirements Cross Reference List, Draft Test Plan, and Draft User's Manual

12

EVERSON

REQUIREMENTS CROSS REFERENCE LIST

While completing the design you must know you haven't forgotten anything; all the specifications or requirements must clearly be satisfied by the design. Obviously some kind of accounting method must be used to keep track of the original specifications while design proceeds. This accounting is accomplished with a separate document that always shows *where* in the design each requirement is satisfied; it is simply a cross reference list that names the requirements that are satisfied by each function, and later, by each computer program or subroutine.

Remember that requirements can split between functions (be part of more than one function). It happens all the time in most designs, especially for fairly general requirements that affect several things. Tests thus have to be broad in scope to verify the satisfaction of such requirements. The traceability of requirements from conception through testing is the most important use of this cross reference document, which is why it is often called the Requirements Traceability Matrix.

A sample for our simulation system functions as given in Chapter 11 is shown in the following example. This matrix must be expanded during development to reference all later development documents.

REQUIREMENTS CROSS REFERENCE LIST

Requirement Paragraph	Function Paragraphs
1.0	3.0, 3.1
1.1	(depends only on actual code)
1.2	2.0, 2.1, 2.11, 2.12, 2.2
1.3	1.1, 1.22
1.4	1.21
1.5	1.1, 1.2, 1.21-1.26, 1.3, 1.31-1.35
1.6	2.0, 2.11, 2.12, 3.0, 4.0
1.7	1.3, 1.31-1.35
1.8	(demonstrable later in design)
1.9	(document to be provided)
2.0	(details not shown in sample functions)
2.1 thru 2.3	(details too voluminous to show in sample functions)
2.4	(not demonstrable at function level)
2.5	(not demonstrable at function level)

THE DRAFT TEST PLAN

To be acceptable, software must work. The developer should be able to show that it is a functioning design. This is so important that the plan for testing is usually begun as soon as the requirements are fully known. At first this plan is little more than an outline of things to be demonstrated by the software in order to satisfy the requirements. As the design proceeds, however, the test plan expands with descriptions of tests that are explicitly related either to different software components or kinds of data. These tests should eventually prove that the software does what it is designed to do.

Building a successful Test Plan requires a good understanding of the design and especially a good grasp of the input and results data for the software. The old "garbage in, garbage out" rule certainly applies to test data. Some method has to be found to certify the reliability of test inputs and to know what the results should be. Thus, because they have the most complete knowledge of how to use the software, the design engineers almost always have the job of assisting testers as the Test Plan nears completion.

Each test usually begins as a statement such as, "With input data described in paragraph AA and the control inputs described in paragraph BB, produce the output data of paragraph CC." This is usually called a *test case*. All of the test cases for a particular piece of software equal the test of that software. As each test case is completed, the paragraph number of the now-satisfied requirement should be noted.

The draft Test Plan for Far-Out Energy Systems' software development is shown in the following example; it corresponds to little more than an enumeration of tests that are suggested by the functional analysis.

(The table of contents of the DoD prescribed Test Plan is shown in Appendix D.)

DRAFT TEST PLAN

1.0 Test of Control Function
    1.1.1 Verify that log-on commands cause predicted system response
    1.1.2 Verify system response to each possible user choice of operation
    1.1.3 Verify correct system response to each input control option
    1.2.1 Verify that correct mode response occurs to each possible user input
    1.2.2 Verify that correct modes of reporting occur in response to user inputs
    1.2.3 Verify that execution paths occurring are those requested

        1.2.4 Verify acceptance of parameters determining operation of the simulation

        1.2.5 Verify that correct statistical analysis of results occurs in response to inputs

        1.2.6 Verify that correct final reports are produced in response to user inputs

        1.3.1 Verify that incompatible data cause the intended error response
        & .2

        1.3.3 Verify error response due to results outside allowable limits

        1.3.4 Verify intended error responses due to incorrect software or hard-
        & .5 ware behavior

    2.0 Test of Data Management Function

        2.1.1 Verify operation of data entry and modification software by
        & .2 checking whether data were entered or modified

        2.2   Operate data base display and reporting software and observe correct performance

    3.0 Observe that user-entered model structure data are converted into the correct internal data in order for the simulation to create the structure of the model

    4.0 Observe that model operational descriptive parameters are correctly converted into internal parameters that are used by the simulation to duplicate model activity

---

DRAFT USER'S MANUAL

For the poor user who is stuck with the software the User's Manual is the only important document. His only prayer of doing something with it is based upon the instruction book. The instruction book (User's Manual) must cover almost everything that can possibly happen. This can be a tall order when the user probably won't have any prior knowledge of the design but can be tremendously eased if the design, in fact, was based on the premise that the software be easy to operate. Thus, a good User's Manual and a good design go hand in hand, each influencing the other; it is for this reason that a draft User's Manual should be written by the time the functional analysis is complete.

Users' needs are so pervasive that they ought to affect the list of requirements. It is important to always remember that most software isn't operated by the people who built it, and as a result, some of it must exist to "hold the user's hand." It also happens that the design effort can turn up *hard spots*, those places where the user could easily make a wrong decision. Conscientious designers then include *virtual requirements*, which lead to improvements in design solely for the users' benefit.

For all of these reasons the User's Manual should be started as early as possible, even if much of it will be rewritten as the design solidifies.

The introductory portion of the document, however, which describes the purpose of the software and the method of achieving it, should change very little.

At the very least, the manual should cover the following topics:

- The purpose of the system including a list of all applications that are known so far
- A general description of the software system, mentioning the major software components that the user will have to deal with, showing how this system fulfills the purpose, and saying what it will (and will not) do with respect to the applications
- A list of interrelated blocks of software and their data flow charts
- A general description of the steps (the order of execution should appear here) necessary to operate the software, including off-line activities such as assembling and organizing data and planning needed results
- Explicit instructions on the steps necessary to use each component of the software, including descriptions of:
  —Input data that are needed and how to enter them
  —Control data and how to enter them
  —Incidental data put out by the software while it executes
  —What to do in response to various error conditions
  —What normal conclusion of execution should produce
- Procedures to follow if the software appears to be performing improperly

A small sample of paragraphs from the first draft of the User's Manual for the small power generators' simulator that is being produced by Far-Out Energy is shown below.

(The table of contents of the DoD prescribed User's Manual is shown in Appendix E.)

SECTION OF DRAFT USER'S MANUAL

3.0 Steps Necessary to Operate the Simulator
   This section outlines all the procedures necessary to run a new set of simulations based upon a new model structure. The steps concerning planning, data gathering, data organization, required preexecution analysis, data entry/verification/update, report specification, control specification, and actual operation of the simulator are included here.

3.1 Planning the Simulation

The purpose of simulating a new model should be clearly established, and a complete list of numerical results to be obtained and the statistical accuracy desired from these results should be included. The plan for the simulation should be signed off by all parties who expect to use the results in order to assure that the simulation will completely satisfy the request. Included in the simulation plan should be a list of all new data items needed and their sources.

3.2 Data Acquisition

Some of the input data may require specific correspondence or literature search. The resulting lead time will require that data acquisition be started well in advance of running the simulation. If provisional (or assumed) values are used for some items, these should be clearly labeled as such. Sources for all items should always be referenced along with accuracies.

3.3 Data Organization and Analysis

Original data from many sources must be converted to a common set of units and put into the input format required by the simulator. Where default values will be used, the placement should be clearly labeled. All data that are used should be on the standard forms for each file (see Section 6); this assures completeness and correct format for entry.

3.4 Data Management

3.4.1 Data Entry

Data files should be created by logging into the system (see Section 4.2), requesting use of the Data Management Subsystem (see Section 4.3) and entering data directly into the files in response to the system commands (see Section 5.2).

3.4.2 Data Verification

After each new file has been filled, verification should be performed by operating the display for that file (see Section 5.4).

3.4.3 Data Update

Incorrect data items should be modified by operating the data update system (see Section 5.3) to insert correct values, followed by redisplay to verify correction.

3.5 Report Specification

This simulation plan's required results should be located in the Report Results Cross Reference List (see Section 7.3) so that needed reports can be identified to satisfy the plan. These reports should be checked off on the Operation Check Sheet (see Section 6.4) as needed control inputs.

3.6 Control Specification

Mode of simulation, model monitoring, and paths specified through the model described in the simulation plan should be checked off on the Operation Check Sheet as needed control inputs.

3.7 Simulator Operation

At this point all data base loading should be complete and verified, and the Operation Check Sheet should contain all needed execution information. The simulator should then be operated by logging in, choosing full-execution operation (see Section 4.5), and entering data on the Operation Check Sheet in response to system commands.

Data Flow and Allocation of Functions to Processes

13

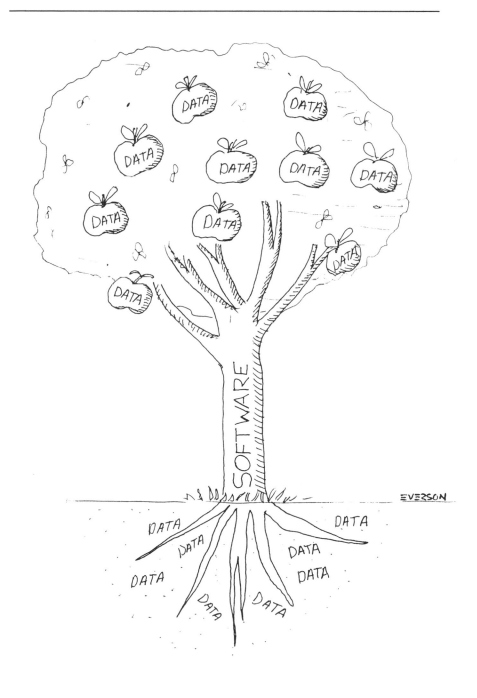

Software both feeds on data and produces data. Software design is therefore permeated by data design. The first step in data design is to decide what the data are; the next step is to show how the data are changed as they are acted upon by the software. Many software designers prefer to make data description and data flow the first thing done in the design process. A newer fashion is to group these topics with functional definitions, describing input, output, and control data for functions. This seems to be a "chicken-and-egg" problem because functions always contain mention of their data; similarly, changes in data always imply functions acting on the data.

All systems appear to fall into one of three classes of data usage:

1. Systems that are mostly dominated by control data and the resultant effects on processing (e.g., command/control systems and data communication systems)
2. Systems that are mostly dominated by the content and structure of their input and output data (e.g., business processing, scientific processing)
3. Systems that are a mixture of the above two types

The first class of system is hard to design by beginning with data flow charts, and the second class is easier to design in this way.

One thing is certain, however; it is necessary to understand the flow of some of the data before processes can begin to be defined. Data flow should be shown at several levels of detail for a large system. There should be a high-level chart showing the whole system, how data are defined, and flow between the major functions. There should also be a chart that displays more detailed data definition and flow within each major function. This partitioning should be done until every defined subfunction is shown with its data on some chart. Most systems of great complexity require that this process of defining data flow and functions be done repetitively. After this has been accomplished the first time for the whole system, go back and do it all over again in greater detail, making use of what was derived in the first attempt.

The successive design at deeper levels of detail is a critical feature of *structured design*, currently the most popular approach in the industry. It is sometimes called *top-down* design because you start at the top level of generality and work your way down in detail. Managers at every level like it because the design can be viewed at the level of detail appropriate to the level of supervision. Presentations to anyone are more likely to succeed this way. The main benefit of detailed data definition is practical, though; it is always possible to start design with general concepts and to "flesh them out" to fill specific needs. This is

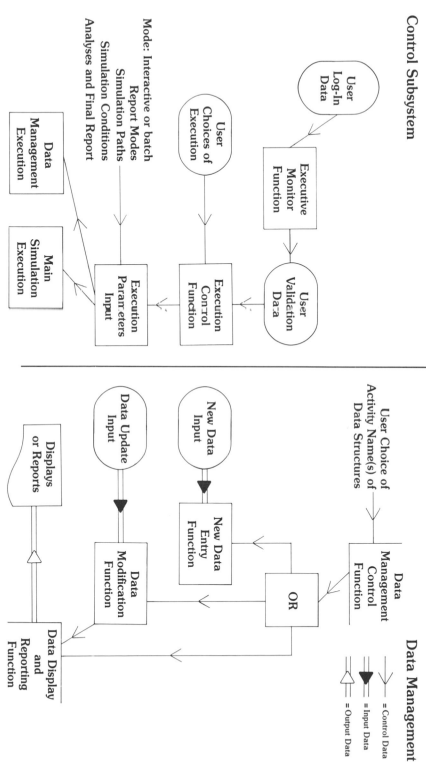

Figure 13.1. Data Flow Chart

FUNCTIONS AND DATA DESCRIPTIONS

Control Subsystem

Executive Monitor Function

Input Data: Only control data
Control Data: All user log-in information such as user name, password
Function Performed: Validation of user access, execution of the next function, the Executive Control Function
Output Data: None (all control data)

Executive Control Function

Input Data: Only control data
Control Data: User choices of simulation
Function Performed: Prompts user to provide forms of execution desired, accepts and stores choices as names of subsystems to be used, causes execution of Executive Parameters Function
Output Data: None (all control data)

Executive Parameters Function

Input Data: Only control data
Control Data: Choices of interactive or batch, report modes, simulation paths, simulation conditions or constraints, types of analysis, and final reports desired.
Function Performed: Prompts user for necessary values of parameters, performs validity checks and calls Error Subsystem for bad data, accepts valid data and stores them, causes Main Simulation Execution or Data Management Control Function when inputs are complete.
Output Data: None (all control data)

Data Management Function

Data Management Control Function

Input Data: Only control data
Control Data: User choice of data entry, data modification or displays or reports, and name(s) of data structures
Function Performed: Prompts user for choice of Data Management Function and name(s) of data structures
Output Data: None (control data only)

New Data Entry Function

Input Data: New data item names and values
Control Data: Exit when done
Function Performed: Performs validity checks on values, calls Error Processing when needed, accepts valid data and stores them, exits upon request
Output Data: None

Data Modification Function

Input Data: Replacement data item names and values
Control Data: Exit when done
Function Performed: Performs validity checks on values, calls Error Processing when needed, accepts valid data items and replaces old items, exits upon request
Output Data: None

Data Display and Reporting Function

Input Data: Only control data
Control Data: Types of reports, names of data structures
Function Performed: Displays or prints reports that were requested
Output Data: Displays or reports

the way the functional analysis was done, and the data flow must organize the functions into a unified whole.

At all points in design the nature of the data is important. A good data flow chart differentiates input, output, and control data for each function. The flow of these should be shown as separate paths, because they fill different roles in the system:

- Control data tell functions what to do (perhaps how to do it).
- Input data are acted upon by a function.
- Output data are what come out of a function.

Within the system the output data of one function are the input (or control) data of other functions. The data flow charts must clearly show these functions for every level of detail. When they also include the hierarchical relations of functions these charts are called HIPO (hierarchy, input, processing, output) charts. They are widely used in the industry.

The completed data versus function flow charts for every major subsystem (for a large system) are often converted into individual descriptions of each function. These are text and constitute the first draft of the major design document, the Computer Program Development Specification. Descriptions of the data input to the whole system from outside and the data flow between major subsystems (*interfaces*) should be included. Each of these descriptions should be at a level of detail that matches that of the function itself.

Figure 13-1 shows the data flow for some of the subsystems outlined in the sample functions listing on page 51, and the text descriptions for those functions are shown on page 62.

ALLOCATION OF FUNCTIONS TO PROCESSES

At last we know enough to define the computer programs. The foregoing discussions prepared the groundwork for knowing what programs are needed and what data they will work on. Now the design of the software itself begins; that is, we talk about computer programs, not more general things.

"The three most important features of a good program are modularity, modularity, and modularity!" This monumental principle should always be followed in defining programs. (What I tell you three times is true.) The concept of modularity gets into the blood of a software designer.

Modularity means that computer programs should only do *one* thing, at whatever level of detail they work. For example, a general-purpose program to accept data from a user and to load it into a file should do only that. However, this program needs to use other sub-programs in order to perform each specific part of its chore:

- To put the user's data values into temporary storage
- To test these data values against allowable limits
- To issue a useful error message about bad data
- To put acceptable data where they belong
- To return to the user any needed information about the status of the system or the files

Modularity lets you use the same subprogram in many different places in your system to accomplish the same kind of thing. This process (whatever it may be) belongs to *one* subprogram (it only has to be designed, coded, debugged, and tested once). Good allocation of functions points out where the same kind of process occurs in different places.

The principle can be rephrased: "Compartment your difficulties and solve each difficulty in a final way." Modularity can be especially useful for those processes that lead to error-prone code such as tricky comparisons and file reading and writing with complicated error response actions.

Extensive modularity leads to a deep hierarchy: the main program will call several subprograms, each subprogram will call several sub-programs, and so on. The system may become several levels deep, but this is as it should be. The lowest level subprograms should be *primitive*, performing functions so simple that they can't be broken down any farther. Thus, the system should consist of nested sub-programs to that point where modularity is achieved at all levels.

If the functions and data flow defined earlier are complete and nonredundant, defining the programs should be straightforward. Con-tinue to use top-down design, first defining high-level programs that most nearly perform the main functions that are already defined. Then define the first level of subprograms that support these main programs as well as the data that flow to and from these subprograms. The second-level of subprograms, which support the first level, should then be defined, etc. Be sure to notice simple subprograms that appear to do *almost* the same thing; where necessary, a few control parameters may take care of the "almost" and save defining a redundant sub-program.

The additional data flow between programs and subprograms will now contain more control data, a result of the hierarchy. Many designers also like to see an additional section in the design document devoted to *interfaces*, the data communication between programs. The individual programs and subprograms (frequently called *modules*)

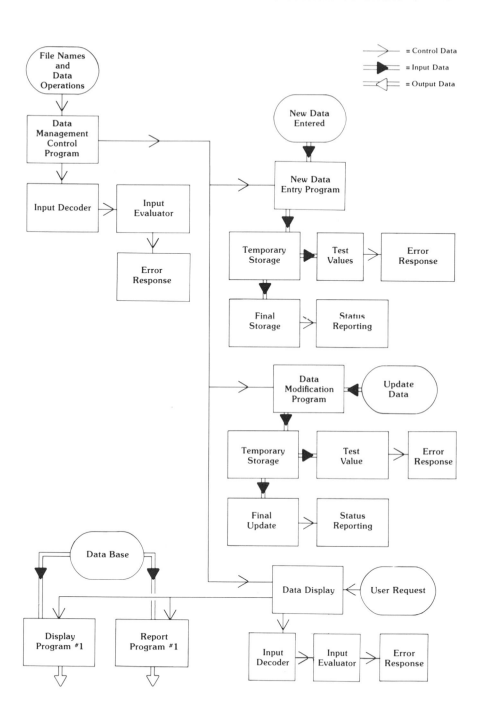

**Figure 13.2. Data and Process Flow for
Data Management Subsystem**

DESCRIPTION OF DATA MANAGEMENT SUBSYSTEM

Data Management Control Program

Input Data: Only control data
Control Data: File names to be accessed and whether they are new data entry, old data modification, or request for displays or reports
Processing: Calls input decoder to translate user request, passes translated request to the requested program in call for requested data activity:
- New data entry program
- Data modification program
- Data display or reporting program

Output Data: Control data to called program

Input Decoder Program

Input Data: Original form of user input data
Control Data: Type of data being decoded
Processing: Decodes input data according to type, calls input evaluator, returns evaluated acceptable data to control program
Output Data: Control data to calling program

Input Evaluator Program

Input Data: Decoded user input data
Control Data: Type of data being evaluated
Processing: Evaluates decoded data as to validity, converts valid data to form of control data, calls error response for invalid data
Output Data: Control data to calling program

New Data Entry Program

Input Data: New data names and values
Control Data: File names
Processing: Calls temporary storage program to test and store data as new
Output Data: Returned status or error messages

Temporary Storage Program

Input Data: New data values
Control Data: New data names
Processing: Calls Test Values Program to test validity of values, calls Error Response Program for bad values
Output Data: Approved data values for these names

Final Storage Program

Input Data: New data values
Control Data: New data names
Processing: Stores values as new data in names, calls Status Reporting Program if needed
Output Data: Status reports if provided

Data Modification Program

Input Data: Data names and update values
Control Data: File names
Processing: Calls Temporary Storage Program to identify data record to be changed, tests validity of data, and replaces old data
Output Data: Returned status or error messages

Final Update Program
Input Data: Replacement data values
Control Data: Data names (including record name)
Processing: Locates old data record, replaces old values with new values,
  calls status reporting if needed
Output Data: Status reports if provided

Data Display Program
Input Data: Only control data
Control Data: Types of display reports, file and data names desired
Processing: Calls Input Decoder Program to decode and evaluate request,
  calls requested Display or Report Programs for valid requests
Output Data: Displays or reports, error responses

Display or Report Programs
Input Data: Requested data base files
Control Data: Report format and content
Processing: Produce displays or reports
Output Data: Displays or reports requested

---

should be described in a simple way concerning input, output, and processing; a chart showing the hierarchy (who calls whom or owns whom) should be prepared. This is called a HIPO description. The set of descriptions, when complete for all functions of all subsystems, is the preliminary design and is contained in the Development Specification document. Since the level of detail is now finer than it was for just a functional description, the data structures are now more precisely defined.

As an example of function expansion into processes, (there is only space for one subsystem) I have chosen data management because of its wide applicability. Figure 13-2 shows the processes associated with the functions of Figure 13-1. The text description of these processes is on page 66.

The Final Detail Design and Program Test Plans

14

DETAIL DESIGN

There should be no unanswered questions about a program when the design is complete. A programmer who is completely familiar with the programming language and method of accessing data should be able to read the design like a book. This implies much more detail than we have shown in the preliminary design, but it does not imply that the function of every line of code be mentioned in the final design.

As discussed earlier in Chapter 5, the two popular ways of presenting the final design are flow charts and design language. Flow charts are not as powerful, so almost everyone now specifies design language for final design. Some design language software aids will format (indent) a listing by using keywords and will cross reference module names and data item names (e.g., Caine, Farber, and Gordon's PDL[1]).

To be effective, more than one design language description should be written. The first attempt should paraphrase the text description of the preliminary design for both programs and data. The second attempt should provide more detail for features that are somewhat vague, and a third (or more) attempt should absolutely "nail down" anything that might be ambiguous. The idea is to write English-language sentences that are almost as specific as code but not quite.

The description should be flexible enough that it can be coded in more than one programming language. This is the best way to learn when design language might be too detailed. Avoiding excessive detail in the design language eliminates the chance that it will have to be pared down or rewritten when the coding is done, possibly by someone who is not as familiar with the program as the original author. The code is supposed to follow the design, but the programmer should be allowed some leeway in deciding exactly how the program is written. That is what programmers are for.

There are portions of the design that should be very detailed in order to avoid last-minute problems. First, data definitions must be very precise for data structures that are common to more than one program. Second, the data communications between programs must be completely defined so that programs are correctly passing and receiving output and inputs.

Data definitions and communications should be defined completely including sequential order, type, size, multiplicity, name, and units. There are two documents that should contain this information: the Data Dictionary, for data base definitions, and the Interface Control Document (ICD), for the data communication definitions. The guiding principle behind this approach is that *shared* design definitions should be nailed down as precisely and as early as possible. A large software design operation is a little like a symphony orchestra: if everyone is to play together, they should be at the same place in the same musical score. When these critical central definitions are not in place, much of the remainder of the design is, in a sense, floating. This frequently results in some parts having to be done over (again, and again!).

Before detail design is actually begun on some types of programs, one should check for the existence of old software that does the same thing. (This is the software version of recycling.) One of the results of modularity should be an accumulation of many programs that do all the simple things. They should *not* have to be written again.[2] (See Chapter 18, page 88.) Usually the problem is being able to find what is needed in huge program libraries with no built-in retrieval capability. Serious thought should be given to keyword and abstract directories (searchability) for archives of software. This is another case of using software to solve software problems.

The design language description of only the top-level program from the description of a data management subsystem (see page 66) is shown on page 71. Notice that this program does almost nothing within itself but calls subprograms to do everything specific. This is modularity—and the more of it the better.

(The DoD prescribed design document includes both preliminary and detail design specifications. Its table of contents is shown in Appendix F, and the table of contents for the data base design specification is in Appendix G.)

PROGRAM TEST PLANS

Each individual module must be tested by the programmer before it can be called complete. The most obvious test is to try the program and to have it work without "fatal" errors. (We don't count compiling the program as a test; that is part of writing it.) The mere fact of successful execution doesn't show in any test plan. From this point on, however, every test the programmer makes should be documented in some standard project format after it succeeds. This set of procedures is called *unit testing*, and its completion leads to the handing over of the program to CM.

DESIGN LANGUAGE DESCRIPTION OF
DATA MANAGEMENT CONTROL PROGRAM

Data Description

Input: Control data below

Control data:

Name	Type	Size	Source	Meaning
Function desired	Characters	6 Characters	Terminal	What will be done
Possible values	NEW (New data entry) UPDATE (Modify old data) REPORT (Produce displays or reports)			
File Name	Characters	7	Terminal	Subject File
Possible values	Any file name in data base			
Evaluation code	Integer	1	Decoder program	Status of request
Possible values	1 = good input 2 = function wrong 3 = bad file name 4 = neither good			
Function flag	Integer	1	Decoder program	OK function
Possible values	1 = NEW 2 = UPDATE 3 = REPORT			
File code	Integer	3	Decoder program	OK file
Possible values	Index into table of files in evaluator program			
Flag	Integer	1	This program	This is the data control program

Program Description

Set evaluation code = 4
Do following input request until "evaluation code" = 1, or at most five times:
    Output request to terminal for function desired, file name
    Accept input values of the above
    Call Input-Decoder Subprogram, passing it the input values, and flag,
    identifying this calling program
    Accept returned values of evaluation code, function flag, file code
    If evaluation code = 4,
        Print "neither function nor file are allowable values" on screen
        Repeat this input request
    Else if evaluation code = 3
        Print "file name not acceptable" on screen
        Repeat this input request
    Else if evaluation code = 2
        Print "function not acceptable" on screen
        Repeat this input request
    Else
        If function flag = 1
            Exit to New Data Entry Program, passing it value of file
            code
        Else if function flag = 2
            Exit to Data Modification Program, passing it value of file
            code
        Else
            Exit to Data Display Program, passing it value of file code
        End if test on function flag
    End if test on evaluation code
End of doing input request
Exit to Executive Control Program
End of Data Management Control Program

TWO TEST CASES FOR DATA MANAGEMENT CONTROL PROGRAM

Test 1: The program responds correctly to bad input data.

Inputs:	Function Desired	File Name
(a)	XXX (bad)	AFILE (a good name)
(b)	NEW (good)	XXX (bad)
(c)	XXX (bad)	XXX (bad)

Control data were the above.

Outputs: Message on terminal identifies bad data type(s).

Criteria: Outputs matched type of bad input.

Requirements: It must be possible to choose desired data program.

Test 2: The program responds correctly to all types of good input data.

Inputs:	Function Desired	File Name
(a)	NEW	AFILE
(b)	UPDATE	BFILE
(c)	REPORT	CFILE

Control data were the above (all good).

Outputs: There were none from this program, but it caused a request for input from the correctly called following program.

Criteria: Correct next program was called and had correct values of file index.

Requirements: It must be possible to choose desired data program.

NOTES

1. Caine, Farber, and Gordon, Inc., PDL, A Program Design Language, Pasadena, CA, 1976.

2. Dr. Sylvan Rubin (a noted contributor to methodology) has pointed out that a serious devotion to reusing software could eventually dramatically reduce the price of software. (private communication)

The Computer Program and Integration and Test Plan   15

THE PROGRAMS

The computer programs should be their own best documents. If all preceding design descriptions were to be lost, it should be possible to understand the programs simply by reading them. The intent of good design is that you will be able to understand the programs, and if a good Standards and Conventions Document has been obeyed, the following elements will be true:

- The programs will be in a readable format, which will tell everything that is local to the programs.
- The programs will match the detail design description very closely.
- There will be adequate comments in the programs to ensure that no code is obscure.

These points are so important that they can completely determine the success or failure of the development all by themselves! For example:

- I know of two projects where the programs were *not* self-documenting; the system had to be thrown away and started afresh (at great cost).
- I have participated in more than two projects where self-documented programs, all by themselves, made it possible to maintain the completed software for years.

Since this book is not intended to contain a course in programming, there is no actual example of a computer program, nor will there be any further detailed discussions about programs. Programming languages differ so much from each other that an example in only one language can really be of little help to everyone.

THE INTEGRATION AND TEST PLAN

Long ago when the preliminary design was done, a draft Test Plan should also have been done. The final form of this plan can be completed once the unit test plans for each program have been submitted.

The System Test Plan is often called an Integration Plan, because the system has to be assembled as one complete unit in order to be tested. This assembly is completed in steps, so that subsystems, made up of *units*, are assembled and tested first. Subsystems are then put together to be tested as a total system.

System integration can be one of the most frustrating stages of the development. It is here that many sins against good design come back to plague the developers. The famous truth, "The whole is equal to the sum of its parts plus their interactions," is now the driving force behind the test results. Any overlooked incompatibilities in the data or processing anywhere in the system will now show up.

This is why the Integration Plan is far more than an administrative requirement. It is serving multiple purposes, all critical to the project:

- It should expose incompatibilities in the data or programs.
- It should specify the stages of assembly for the system so that the diagnosis of any trouble remains simple.
- It should clearly show the requirements that are satisfied by each test case during system assembly.

Remember, this set of tests is the developer's way of proving that the system is finished.

The Integration and Test Plan can only be successful if it is written by a designer who has a complete understanding of the entire system. The more elements that are tested at once, the more knowledge that is required to interpret the results. Integration and testing is frequently supervised by someone who has been in constant touch with the design activity. This person may have written the original draft Test Plan and perhaps also the final version. The reason for the Test Plan being started early is to allow it to keep pace with the design and to include tests of functions as they are identified; thus an understanding of how to test the system will grow in parallel with the progress of the design.

The final Test Plan document will usually be 100 or so pages in length and will go into a great amount of detail. No attempt will be made here to present an example of the final Test Plan; abstracting portions of it would misrepresent the comprehensive nature of the document. (See Appendix D for the DoD prescribed Test Plan table of contents and Appendix H for the contents of its matching Test Analysis Report.)

A Software Maintenance Manual and a User's Manual   16

EVERSON

MAINTENANCE MANUAL

Software can act as if it is "broken," just the same as a machine; thus it should be possible to repair it, just as you would a machine. Repairing software requires an instruction book analogous to the shop manual for a machine. The *troubleshooting* of software malfunctions is more like an intellectual puzzle than hardware repair, and this manual consists mostly of descriptions of how to find out what is wrong. The manual is in fact written when you don't think *anything* is wrong.

The Maintenance Manual must provide a step-by-step formula for locating problems within a software system. The most important step, though, is to know the difference between a hardware problem and a software problem. In a mixed hardware-software system two Maintenance Manuals are required, one for hardware and one for software. Once the problems are localized to software, however, the prescribed test procedures should involve various error diagnostics, in conjunction with data cases that can cause the errors, to pinpoint which part of the software is incorrectly structured. The actual software design for this part must then be referenced to discover exactly how to fix it. The fixing actually consists of (we hope) minor redesign and rewriting of the offending software. One should realize that these problems are just as likely to be due to data definitions as they are to bugs in the programs; in this case only the data definitions would require changing.

Obviously, the manual should tell how to recompile the changed programs or data definitions or should refer to available vendor manuals in a very explicit way. *All* steps in replacing the faulty software should be covered in detail:

- Using error diagnostics and test data to locate the problem
- Finding the design documents that describe the faulty software
- Identifying the place where the design change(s) must be made
- Modifying the design in accordance with standards and conventions
- Rewriting the program(s) or data definition(s) according to the new design
- Recompiling the result
- Creating the new executable (object code) library based upon the new code
- Testing all over again to prove that the problem is fixed *and* that no new problems have been created
- Satisfying existing CM requirements associated with the changes

Since there is not enough space here to show a representative example of a Maintenance Manual, only a sample Table of Contents is presented. The typical contents based on the items listed above is represented on page 79. (The DoD prescribed Maintenance Manual table of contents is shown in Appendix I.)

THE USER'S MANUAL

The draft User's Manual generated early in the project (see page 57) contained references to a simulation request plan and various check sheets. These forms should simplify operation of the system and improve productivity by ensuring that all needed data are available and that the required results are clearly defined. These forms are part of the completed User's Manual that is required to attend delivery of the software.

It is obvious that the complete system Test Plan would be much easier to prepare if the User's Manual were finished first. In a sense the testers are the first real users of the system (they are different from the developers). Feedback from testers who work from the User's Manual can usually much improve its utility before final editing. This is yet another example of the organic nature of software development—the different aspects complement and support each other when given the chance.

**MAINTENANCE MANUAL TABLE OF CONTENTS
FOR SMALL POWER GENERATORS SIMULATOR**

Section I   Error Diagnostics: Code ID and Message
   1. System-Level Errors
   2. Control-Parameter Errors
   3. Data Base Management Errors
   4. Incompatible Simulation Structure Errors
   5. Incompatible Simulation Function Errors
   6. Simulation Execution Errors
   7. Output Data Errors
   8. Report Production Errors
Section II   Design Description Cross Reference Listings Versus Error Codes
   1. Control Subsystem
   2. Data Base Management Subsystem
   3. Simulation Structuring Subsystem
   4. Simulation Execution Subsystem
   5. Statistical Analysis Subsystem
   6. Reporting and Display Subsystem
Section III Directory to Design Documents
Section IV   Summary of Standards and Conventions for Redesign and Coding
Section V   Compilation of Programs
Section VI   Library Regeneration
Section VII Test and Validation Criteria
Section VIII Configuration Management Requirements for Maintenance

---

The User's Manual is usually quite a thick book, because it has to give advice not only on what to do but also on what *not* to do. It has to anticipate the almost total unfamiliarity that a new user will have with the system. Far-Out Energy's User's Manual Table of Contents of their completed manual is on page 80 (see page 57 for sample section). (The DoD equivalent is shown in Appendix E.)

**USER'S MANUAL TABLE OF CONTENTS
FOR SMALL POWER GENERATORS SIMULATOR**

The Phases of Software Development

Producing the Foundations of the Project

17

The project is begun by "designing the project itself." Design of the project is contained in the project documents:

- The schedule
- The Software Development Plan
- The Configuration Management Plan
- The Standards and Conventions Document
- The Quality Assurance Plan

The basis of the work described in these documents is given in the Requirements and Specifications Document.

These documents define what will be done, who will do it, how it will be done, and when various things will be finished. Fortunately, the first five documents usually have fairly standard contents (see Chapters 6-9), but they must be specifically written to describe *this* project. The Requirements and Specifications Document uniquely describes what is to be developed in this project.

The schedule and the Software Development Plan should be devised in parallel, with a first guess at critical paths deciding the order of achieving milestones. The training requirements should be settled first so that these needs can be approached immediately. Personnel assignments also have high priority, especially of those individuals who will complete the initial documents. The software development manager and those who report directly to him are closely involved with the writing of these documents. The schedule and the development plan don't require intimate familiarity with the nuts and bolts of the project, so the engineers need not be heavily tied up with this writing.

That's good, because the engineers are needed to write the Requirements and Specifications Document. The software designers and senior programmers are obligated to finish critical sections of the Standards and Conventions Document—the glossary of system terminology and the naming conventions—before design can begin. This leaves the Configuration Management Plan and the Quality Assurance Plan to the administrative experts most familiar with these activities.

If the development is on a computer system new to most of the staff, the CM procedures may require that special adaptations to the management software be provided by the vendor. By the time the Requirements Document is finished, the components of the software identified as *configuration items* should be established. Work on the development is allocated to these configuration items. They are the "building blocks" referenced in the Schedule and Development Plan. Thus they should be defined so that these other documents can be completed. It should be noted that the administrative division of the system into configuration items may not correspond to the logical division of the system into subsystems. Sometimes a configuration item may be more than one subsystem (if the subsystems are small enough); sometimes a big subsystem may consist of several configuration items.

This phase of the project should culminate in everyone using a common terminology for the system and agreeing on the "ground rules" for the development. There are some variations in the industry on the other things that may be done in this phase. For example, it is quite common to identify software subsystems of the main system and to allocate requirements to them in the Requirements Document. This is already a small step in design, but in large systems it may be a big help in organizing everyone's thoughts about the system.

Officially defined phases of software design are certified as complete by design reviews. The names and definitions of these reviews may vary slightly with different developers and customers, but government-purchased development specifies a certain minimum number of such reviews. Currently, these are:

- The System Requirements Review, which takes place at the end of this initial development phase
- The Preliminary Design Review, which terminates the function definition phase
- The Critical Design Review, which evaluates the completed design

The purpose of each of these reviews is to present the completed work of the phase and to obtain customer approval of the results. The approved design material is called a baseline for that review. This design material obviously includes all the documents prepared during that development phase, but the presentation requires even more material. A small project will require a half-day presentation, a big project up to three or four days! Obviously the presentation involves elaborate preparation.

The presentation for the System Requirements Review might consist of the following topics:

- Agenda and introduction of speakers
- Overview of the system

- Relations between hardware, software, and operation components
- Definitions of configuration items (and possibly subsystems)
- Schedule for milestones on configuration items
- Categories of requirements
- Assignment of requirements to categories
- Performance requirements (quantitative)
- Computer system requirements
- Development methodology
- Simulations
- Presentations of plans and documents (in outline form)
- Summary and discussion

It is sensible to give the audience a chance to be well informed. Therefore, the printed copy that supports this agenda should be distributed at least two weeks before the meeting (for large projects, two months before). It is intended that the reviewer evaluate this material beforehand and submit written questions well in advance of the meeting. Then the answers to these questions will have been prepared by the time of the meeting. If this procedure is truly honored, almost everyone at the review will understand the background material and what the problems are. The design review would then serve the function of two meetings: the first to explain the topic and to inform everyone and the second to discuss it and agree on the design.

Unfortunately, most of the audience is usually too busy with other things to review the material in advance, so much of the presentation is often devoted to educating people who should have done their homework. Some organizations have a cadre of experts at such reviews, who are themselves taught the subject matter; they then present much of the overview and high-level material (leaving the details to the people who worked on them). This leads to reviews with a smooth, professional touch and frees technical people to concentrate on what they are most concerned with. Regretfully, though, this is a luxury that only large firms can afford.

Problems raised at the design review are assigned to ad hoc working groups or to individuals for solution; such problems are not included in the approved baseline of the design material. This baseline, agreed upon by customer and vendor, represents the foundation upon which the next phase of the design will be built.

Generating the Functional Description and Data Flow   **18**

The actual design (as contrasted from set up) now begins. All the groundwork has finally been laid for both procedures and description of the job. The major contributors to the design are the engineers, who, chances are, are not software people at all. If the software being developed is for hardware control or testing, many of these engineers may be real "nuts-and-bolts" people. The whole functional design phase probably evolved out of the need to use standard engineering approaches (and people) for software design. A hybrid breed of engineer has grown up in the last twenty years called a *system engineer* in most software groups. Such an individual can be an engineer, a physical scientist, a mathematician, anyone who has adapted to software. The function descriptions are usually the responsibility of these system engineers who work with hardware engineers or specialists on the application.

Suddenly a new talent becomes crucial to the project: the ability to communicate. Not only must the engineering staff understand what the developed system must do, they must be able to show this to everyone else. The problem is frequently serious, because many technical people can't express themselves very well. At this stage of the project, in order to guarantee understanding, some kind of formalized technical descriptive method is usually beneficial. This can be nothing more than a standards and conventions check list that the engineers would be made to follow in their functional descriptions and data flow charts. It could even be an official part of the Standards and Conventions Document. Here is where the prior evolution of a good glossary and naming convention pays off.

The "pure" software people are not sitting out this part of the project. Part of the functional analysis is to identify standard software functions that will clearly be used to do common things (input, output, display of errors, general system control, etc.). These functions are normally called *utilities*, but they are really just general-purpose software. Specifying what general-purpose software is needed has to be done at this stage of the project (or earlier, if it is to be treated as a configuration item, and should be scheduled separately).

A big software shop accumulates a lot of this stuff over the years, and they should be able to recycle much of it (see Chapter 14, page 70). A newcomer, however, must design and write it or buy it. Creative thought should be devoted to isolating general-purpose software, because the benefits are huge:

- The burden of designing and coding repetitive activities can be lifted out of the development, solved once, and tested to death so that everyone can use it.

- By segregating often-used software functions first, the rest of the design can be limited to almost purely application-specific programs. This means that right at the start modularity has been made easier to achieve.

- Because this utility software is usually simple to design and to code, programmers can begin work on it immediately, while the rest of the system is still being designed.

- General-purpose software can be reused for other projects, if properly documented for retrieval and carefully designed to interface with a wide variety of programs.

- Sometimes a lot of general-purpose software can be bought in the form of Data Management Systems, special Executive Operating Systems, sorting and file-management utilities, report-generating systems, etc. This advantage is more important than it seems, because it is almost *always* cheaper to buy off-the-shelf software than it is to build and test it. Besides, everyone is getting tired of "reinventing the wheel."

The data flow descriptions will naturally be worked out in parallel with the functional descriptions. If the system works entirely from a centralized pool of data (is data base-driven), the data flow will dominate the functional description. (It is fashionable to specify this kind of system in the Statement of Work.) The requirement of a common data base for the entire system has a unifying effect on the design. It means that when the functional description is finished, the data base description must be finished. The software designers then know what *all* the data are that they have to work with. The interfaces between functions are fully specified (input-function-output), and the functions will all be allocated by subsystems.

Meanwhile, someone familiar with user needs should be producing a draft User's Manual that is based on the functional design. As mentioned earlier, there is an interaction between a good User's Manual and a good functional design; they should move along together during this phase. Also being produced at this time is a draft Test Plan and the requirements cross references to the functions, upon which the Test

Plan is based. These documents frequently are just well-developed outlines at this stage, but they are needed to make sure that nothing which needs testing is overlooked.

Obviously, all the people simultaneously working on these related efforts need to keep in touch. (This is when the copy machine begins to get overworked.) For a larger project, keeping the critical paths on schedule (tracking the correlated work) requires more attention. The people who are performing critical tasks discover they are spending too much time in meetings or writing status reports. If there is a hardware component being developed along with the software, all these tracking problems ultimately depend on the hardware design being frozen before the software design begins. Any failures in the hardware project have a serious impact on the related parts of the software project.

Some developers limit the preliminary design phase to functional and data descriptions and the accompanying elements that have been discussed. However, the more common practice is to also identify the software components, as the last step in preliminary design. As described earlier the functions are mapped onto software processes in a hierarchical manner. This first step in software definition doesn't necessarily involve a greater specification of detail; it is simply a giant step toward having a basic picture of the whole system. The design document produced in this phase is called the Computer Program Design Specification (or Design Specification). The results of the work to date are presented in the Preliminary Design Review, thus concluding the preliminary work phase. The agenda for the review, analogous to the System Requirements Review in its approach, might contain the following topics:

- Agenda and introduction of speakers
- Overview and objectives of this part of the design
- Review of outline of the requirements
- High-level functions within each subsystem (subsystem definition if not previously done)
- Categories of functions across all subsystems
- Functions assigned to general-purpose software
- Hierarchical analysis of functions by subsystem
- Data flow between subsystems
- Data flow within subsystems
- Assignment of software components to functions
- Assignment of requirements to functions
- Outline of Test Plan
- Outline of User's Manual
- Summary and discussion

The general practices advised earlier for the requirements review are true for all of the review processes (see Chapter 17, page 84). The successful Preliminary Design Review will result in the preliminary design baseline of documents, which contains the approved design. Points of contention or undecided items remain as open questions until ad hoc groups settle them to everyone's satisfaction. There should be very few of these—the design can't proceed much farther with large holes in the plan. A baseline that has too many "to-be-decided" (TBD) items is a snare and a delusion of progress. No customer should put up with it and no developer should try to get away with it. An incomplete preliminary design baseline drives software designers crazy and makes the remaining schedule hard to interpret and to follow. It is far better to bite the bullet and allow the schedule for the Preliminary Design Review to slip than to make do with an incomplete one. Only the most sound and totally complete design is an adequate basis for the rest of the design process.

The Final Design Phase   19

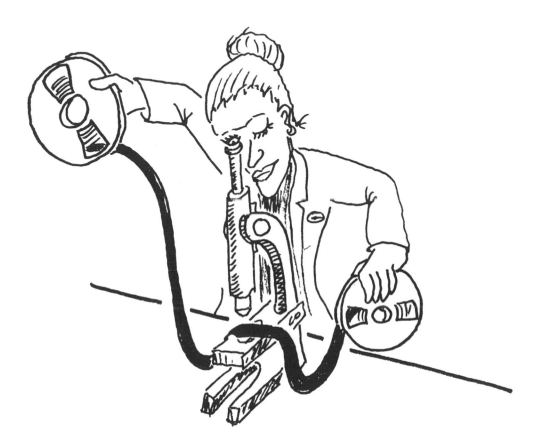

From now on work should be focused strictly on the software. The engineering had better be complete, or the design will be held back until it catches up. The design specification should prescribe what the purpose, input, output, and control data of each computer program are. It usually won't describe exactly how the program's purpose should be achieved; this is the business of the final development phase.

Lots of details have to be worked out. Everything mentioned in the preliminary design specification about data structures or data items has to be made completely explicit. Any sections of the Standards and Conventions Guide that are still in draft form must be completely finished and approved, and a highly detailed description of the processing in each program is naturally provided. As part of these descriptions, the detailed data communications between programs (the interfaces) are described.

The technical leadership of the design activity switches from engineers to senior programmers and systems analysts. They were previously occupied in making sure that the functional design is compatible with the intended computer system. Some of the software staff were fully assigned to designing and coding general-purpose software, well in advance of the specific application coding.

Technical leadership is now especially important to the success of the project. Much of the final design will, of necessity, be done by programmers or analysts who have a limited grasp of hardware capabilities. They might easily specify processing that is grossly inefficient, because the code was easy to write this way. A critical role of the project leaders is to review the final design as it progresses. This is achieved by a review, a *design walkthrough*. As the designers produce their design language descriptions (or flow charts), they are reviewed by a group of other designers led by a senior analyst. They should agonize over all the consequences of the design presented. This doesn't mean they should redesign it, only that it should "pass muster" based on all the criteria of good design:

- Efficiency of processing
- Economical data storage
- Clarity of the design language
- Modularity of the software components
- Testability of the steps in processing
- Satisfaction of the standards and conventions for design

These walkthroughs, plus the final Critical Design Review, are the major insurance of excellence in the product. A member of the QA team (see Chapter 8, page 36) should always be present at a walkthrough; there should be few nasty surprises for the QA people during their final review of the design.

There are limitations to what can be achieved in even the best design document. Unless the system being built is very simple (or the staff consists of geniuses), there will be some real flaws in the written design, usually some overlooked (or unforseeable) problem in writing an acceptable program. It is tolerated in most cases only because the programmer interpreting the design is smart enough to work around it. Better insurance against such flaws, though, is to have the senior analyst who supervised the design available to rework it. There is no substitute for continuity of responsibility on a project!

Detail design, the final design phase, is the finish of everything except coding, integrating, and testing. This means that draft versions of the requirements cross reference to programs, the Test and Integration Plan, the Maintenance Manual, and User's Manual all must be in final form. Also, the coding section of the Standards and Conventions Guide is now due. The systems engineers, whose responsibilities are now much smaller, are usually saddled with the final editing of these documents.

The culminating design review, the Critical Design Review, has a vast amount of detail to cover, and advance distribution of the materials is especially important. By this time roughly 60 percent of the project budget should have been spent, and great importance is placed on getting final design approval immediately after the review. It pays (literally) to do a good job on the review.

The general practices described for the previous two review stages still hold true (see Chapter 17, page 84). A sample agenda might look like the following:

- Agenda and introduction of speakers
- Overview and objectives
- Review of outline of the requirements
- Review of software components
- Hierarchical organization of programs
- Organization of the data base and its size
- Top-level design language description of subsystems
- Prominent design decisions made in this phase
- Estimates of performance
- Estimates of computer resource usage (including sizes of data and programs)
- Flexibility for future development
- Limitations of the design
- The Integration and Test Plan
- The Maintenance and User's Manuals
- Implementation of quality assurance
- Status of the schedule

Hopefully, there will be very few undecided points requiring later sign off. The so-called critical design baseline that is approved will be turned over to CM for housekeeping, and changes to *any* documents approved at this time subsequently require review and approval by special review boards. The *code-to* design has become a delivered product, along with its companion documents. The next product to be delivered is the software itself.

Producing the Software   20

All the project activity has finally come to a focus. With only some 20 percent of the total time spent on the project available to them, the programmers are now expected to write and debug all of the programs (that's right, only 20 percent!). It is thought to take so little time because much of the thinking is supposedly already done. This is the big difference between software system development and what is scornfully called "hobby-shop programming." The first involves finishing the design and then coding, and the second is designing as you code. Only a very small system, created by at most two programmers, is likely to have an acceptable design if it is done using this "seat-of-the-pants" approach. However, big systems that are in trouble often end up being finished this way. Too bad! Sometimes they are not finished, because the customer realizes what kind of product he is getting.

The technical leadership mentioned previously should continue to monitor the code being written. No one is perfect, not even an experienced programmer. The structured walkthrough review of code is the method used by the senior staff to assure quality. As programs are finished (but not debugged), small groups of programmers and designers agonize over the actual code, as they did over the design. The writer of the code almost always benefits from the suggestions given, and everyone usually learns something. Adherence to the standards and conventions is automatically demonstrated, and any departures from the design must be shown to be improvements. QA people attend all walkthroughs and make notes.

These code walkthroughs should always be done *before* an attempt has been made to debug, because the harsh fact is that debugging code takes three times as long (at least!) as writing it. Hopefully, this has been accounted for in the schedule. It is possible that a program may go through two or more versions before being judged worthy of continuation through debugging.

Debugging skill is what most distinguishes amateurs from professionals. It has been found that very small children can be taught how to write programs, but very few can debug the programs they write. The problem is fundamental: When you finish writing a program you think there is nothing wrong with it. When it doesn't work, though, you have to review the whole design, your belief in how the language works, and find something to question. If a few simple changes don't work, you have to install temporary code that prints out values of the data used in all stages of the processing. Examination of this diagnostic data will usually show what is wrong, but, if not, what then?

Fortunately, there are debugging aids available for common languages on most computers. These are programs that can monitor the processing in a subject program and can trap errors (show where they occurred in the code). Since no one has figured out how to write perfect programs the first time, we all learn to live with debugging. The structured walkthroughs have been a big help in exposing all but the most obscure errors in most programs.

During this coding period, *implementation*, it becomes increasingly clear whether the project schedule will allow for everything to be done properly. In almost all projects the schedule is holy, but many elements of the documentation are not. If the project is behind schedule, management looks around for corners to be cut. The software has to be delivered and satisfy the requirements, but there is always room for adjustments in the written text material and the amount of testing that is done. These sins of omission will eventually have to be dealt with. It may be the end user, who can't understand a sloppily written manual, or, more likely, a maintenance programmer, who has to fix hurriedly written and poorly tested code with few (or no!) comments. If the speed up of the project occurs after a good final design exists, the consequences can be less disastrous; this is especially true if the same people who created the design are also implementing it. It is perfectly possible to sabotage a project by moving its expert people out onto another project that is short-handed. This can be forestalled by having a software development plan that commits these people through the project (but such a commitment can always be broken).

Another consequence of being behind schedule is management's need for more frequent reassurance of project status. If this is allowed to take implementers away from their work, it obviously makes the project even more behind schedule. It is wise to have work leaders who buffer the programmers from the schedule tracking-and-reporting activities, because many software people are antagonized by the concerns of a suffering management.

Unit testing, the last step in implementation, shows that all the most-used paths through a program yield correct results. The programmer usually fills out a form that describes each case:

- Names of the input data and their test values
- What the processing does
- Names of the output data and their correct values

Following this, the program is run, and the annotated program I/O sheets are attached to each test case sheet to show that things worked.

When all of the test cases work, the program is delivered to CM and the test cases to the test group. The program is now controlled, and any changes to it require reviews and approvals. When all of the programs are so delivered, the implementation phase is complete.

Integration and Testing 21

System integration is a little like playing a brand new symphony for the first time. The conductor's score is probably analogous to the documents describing who owns whom (the hierarchy chart) and what data are passed to whom (the interface document). These documents are obviously being tested for correctness along with the software. Features of the computer's own software may be used differently for integration than they were for unit testing (e.g., the executable object code may be loaded into libraries or link edited differently). This can lead to surprising results when the integrated programs execute, unless the integration director understands such things. It emphasizes the need for a "chief integrator" who understands a lot about the whole system being integrated and the computer's operating software. Frequently such a person has been involved with the design of the project software Executive Control System, where all the subsystems get their directions from users.

This Executive Control System (all systems have one) is usually the first subsystem to be integrated, primarily because it has the highest content of general-purpose software and is most likely to be finished first. Many systems are designed so that this system separately exercises the next lower level of subsystem (first subsystem A, then B, etc.). If so, then these subsystems can be integrated individually, in parallel, by separate groups and, as they are finished, integrated one by one with the executive system.

The details of these integration and test procedures should be delivered as part of the Integration Plan at the end of the final design. Also, the data bases necessary to carry out integration should be assembled and installed according to a schedule prescribed in this plan. If possible, some procedure for testing the correctness of test data bases should have been worked out. The tested data bases should be available at the start of integration.

Most of the integration is performed after the programmers have finished their programs. Thus, many of the software staff are available to assist the permanent integration and test team. It is particularly helpful to assign programmers to integrate subsystems that contain some code they developed. The expertise acquired during design and coding is invaluable in diagnosing the results of integration or test failures.

Deficiencies will show up all during integration which require modifications to the software. This is merely an extension of debugging to the full-scale system. These bugs may be much harder to identify because they are embedded in such large amounts of code (the whole system, in many cases). Once discovered, however, the defective code is recycled back to the author-programmer for correction. All requests for changes and their responses are embedded in the configuration control process. The CM team is busy preparing new baselines for the system, so integration is always being done on the best version.

This may be a hectic time for the development staff because everyone is confronting the consequences of all the work that is involved with designing and coding the system. Here again, the presence of people who did the early work can iron out many problems. The Maintenance Manual for the software should already be coming into use by the integrators; it too is being debugged, as is the User's Manual.

Gradually, test cases will begin to routinely succeed for all of the variations specified in the test input data. When all test cases have safely been finished successfully, that version of the system, the test baseline, is pronounced ready for customer delivery. This baseline is not necessarily the final version of the system, unless it is only going to be used by the customer on the developer's computer (which may be true for certain analytic software). The customer may also run his own acceptance tests on his computer, before permanently installing the software in the *operational configuration*.

Many developers regard the installed, operational software as still being "developed" in this last phase, even though by this time it is accepted and paid for and the development staff is working on other projects. There may be a maintenance staff provided on a long-term basis by the developer of the system, but this is not really considered a part of the development process. We have chosen to say that integration and testing is really the last time when the whole crew may be involved in the development process, so it is essentially the last phase of development.

The integration and testing phase is very different in rigor for different kinds of software. Real-time command-and-control software *has* to work almost perfectly to protect (sometimes) multimillion dollar systems (or people, as in the APOLLO moon landings). You can imagine how thoroughly such software must be tested before its final installation and how much more expensive this makes its development. Much more relaxed is the acceptance of software that will be operated for the customer by some of the same staff who developed it (e.g., for custom computation or computer simulation studies).

The stricter guidelines for testing will appear all the way back down the line during development in the form of higher standards for design and coding excellence. This is why so much variability may be encountered in the enforcement of software development practices and the level of detail expected in software documents.

We shouldn't sign off without telling how Far-Out Energy Systems succeeded on its project. It did pretty well (for a newcomer) at producing good documentation and on schedule and at meeting good standards. Its design led to good modular programs, but its best expert was transferred to another project before integration was complete. This caused integration and testing to get three weeks behind schedule—no one else understood system bugs as they showed up. So they transferred their expert back to the simulation project in order to finish testing and to deliver the software, so it all had a happy ending. (They were only three weeks late and didn't exceed project budget.) Everyone learned a lot, and they are already bidding on another software project.

Epilogue

The main features of software engineering have been condensed into just a few pages. Most of these pages are extensive descriptions of how to write various documents. As one "old-timer" puts it, "Most of what we produce is paper"—and this is probably true. Even the software itself must exist on paper as programs and data definitions. All of this paper should be supporting a finely tuned, complex mechanism: the project organization. Complexity often breeds complexity, and most industrial software requires a complex activity to produce it.

The development plans, schedules, standards, controls, and reviews have been shown to serve necessary purposes. There are few forms of engineering that are more creative which also demand that a budget and schedule be met and that the product must work right. This is what all the administrative and design documentation should guarantee. It should be clear now why writing a lot of computer programs is *not* the biggest part of software development and why software now costs several times what its host computer costs.

I have tried to "tell it like it is" for the art of software development, but throughout the industry there are variations in terminology and when and how certain things are done. One Golden Rule always holds true, it seems: Define what the software will do, then design it *completely* before coding it.

But there are exceptions even to this. What do you do if the users-to-be of the software don't have enough knowledge of their application to know completely what the software should do, but they still want it? They want a software system to be able to do some things but also have an open-ended quality so that the system can grow. It's a tough design problem. Some developers have approached this with a drastic solution: Be prepared to do the development twice:

- The first system developed should be a full-scale prototype, intended to give experience to the users. It is a test bed and will essentially be thrown away when people have learned from it.

- The second system will incorporate requirements that were unknown when the first system was designed. The design staff will have experience with this kind of system. The second version will be shaken down even before it is designed.

The above approach is harder to sell, but if requirements are incomplete or fuzzy, is may be cost effective. It is the only kind of design-as-you-go software that is based on solid experience.

Another kind of software that bypasses the earlier-mentioned Golden Rule is created by an Applications Program Generator, software that is semiautomatically generated by software. That is, someone has built a "smart" program that can write software, using the requirements statements as input data. A lot of business data processing can be handled by Applications Program Generators, and their use will grow with accumulated experience. They are *not* simple to design or cheap to implement, but they may be the wave of the future.

Appendix A

DEPARTMENT OF DEFENSE
FUNCTIONAL DESCRIPTION
TABLE OF CONTENTS

Appendix B

**DEPARTMENT OF DEFENSE DATA
REQUIREMENTS DESCRIPTION
TABLE OF CONTENTS**

Appendix C

Appendix D

DEPARTMENT OF DEFENSE TEST PLAN
TABLE OF CONTENTS

Appendix E

DEPARTMENT OF DEFENSE USER'S MANUAL
TABLE OF CONTENTS

Appendix F

DEPARTMENT OF DEFENSE
PROGRAM SPECIFICATION
TABLE OF CONTENTS

Appendix G

**DEPARTMENT OF DEFENSE
DATA BASE SPECIFICATION
TABLE OF CONTENTS**

Appendix H

**DEPARTMENT OF DEFENSE TEST ANALYSIS REPORT
TABLE OF CONTENTS**

Appendix I

DEPARTMENT OF DEFENSE
PROGRAM MAINTENANCE MANUAL
TABLE OF CONTENTS

Appendix J

PROGRAM DESIGN LANGUAGE DESCRIPTION OF THE SOFTWARE DEVELOPMENT PROCESS

This is a design description of a system development methodology written in a system design language. The purpose is twofold: (1) to precisely define a particular system development process and (2) to demonstrate the flexibility of the design language, ATHENA.

This system development design is defined here only for its higher-level processes. Its further elaboration would depend partly on the types of system to be developed and on the resources and policies of the organization performing the development work. In this particular demonstration, the system design procedure defined here specifies how to extend itself to meet any externally defined requirements.

System Development =

Develop specifications, preliminary design, detail design, implement, test

Develop Specifications =

Analyze initial requirements, produce system specs

Produce System Specs =

Develop initial specifications, loop [identify derived requirements, check req's vs functional specs, if <all req's met> exit loop, revise functions specs]

Preliminary Design =

loop [design system data structures, design system processes, verify functional correctness of design]

Design System Data Structures =

loop [write data structure definitions, evaluate definitions, expand data definitions hierarchically]

Design System Processes =

Write initial top-level process definitions, loop [tasks [expand process definitions, insert data references, test for functional correctness], evaluate whether detailed enough]

Verify Functional Correctness of Design =

loop [check functional specs vs prelim. design, alt <design satisfied all functional specs> exit [preliminary design]/rework the design elements that do not meet functional specs]

Detail Design =

Allocate design processes to system modules, produce detail designs

Allocate Design Processes to System Modules =

tasks [identify available modules that fit design, identify modules to be designed and implemented, adjust module interfaces to minimize new module development], allocate modules to CPCI and CPC groups

Produce Detail Designs =

loop (all modules [if <module is existing one> [choose proper parameters, cycle], determine whether new module should be designed to be reusable, design interface, design executable code, document module, if <to be reusable> [document parameters and properties of module in detail, add to module catalog]]

—S. Rubin
Los Altos Hills, CA
November 1982

Bibliography

The following books are recommended for those who wish to further explore the field of software engineering.

Boehm, Barry W. 1981. *Software Engineering Economics*, Englewood Cliffs, NJ: Prentice-Hall.

Tonies, Charles C. and Jensen, Randall W. 1979. *Software Engineering* Englewood Cliffs, NJ: Prentice-Hall.

Brooks, Frederick, Jr. 1975. *The Mythical Man-Month*. New York: Yourdon.

Weinberg, Gerald M. 1971. *The Psychology of Computer Programming*. New York: Van-Nostrand Reinhold.

Kernighan, Brian W. and Plauger, P. J. 1974. *The Elements of Programming Style*. New York: Yourdon.

———.1978. *Software Tools*. New York: Yourdon.